SO-DTC-275

You've Got Style!

Les Christie

Scott Holmgren

David C. Cook Publishing Co.
Elgin, Illinois—Weston, Ontario

Custom Curriculum
You've Got Style!

© 1993 David C. Cook Publishing Co.

Unless otherwise noted, Scripture quotations are from the Holy Bible, New International Version (NIV), © 1973, 1978, 1984 by International Bible Society. Used by permission of Zondervan Bible Publishers.

Published by David C. Cook Publishing Co.
850 North Grove Ave., Elgin, IL 60120
Cable address: DCCOOK
Series creator: John Duckworth
Series editor: Randy Southern
Editor: Lorraine Triggs
Option writers: John Duckworth, Nelson E. Copeland, Jr., and Ellen Larson
Designer: Bill Paetzold
Cover illustrator: Rob Barber
Inside illustrator: Al Hering
Printed in U.S.A.

ISBN: 0-7814-5006-3

CONTENTS

Sessions by Scott Holmgren
Options by John Duckworth, Nelson E. Copeland, Jr., and Ellen Larson

About the Authors

Scott Holmgren is a free-lance writer. A graduate of Columbia College in Chicago, Scott lives in Wheaton, Illinois.

John Duckworth is a writer and illustrator in Carol Stream, Illinois. He has worked with teenagers in youth groups and Sunday school, written several books including *The School Zone* (SonPower), and created such youth resources as *Hot Topics Youth Electives* and *Snap Sessions* for David C. Cook.

Nelson E. Copeland, Jr. is a nationally known speaker and the author of several youth resources including *Great Games for City Kids* (Youth Specialties) and *A New Agenda for Urban Youth* (Winston-Derek). He is president of the Christian Education Coalition for African-American Leadership (CECAAL), an organization dedicated to reinforcing educational and cultural excellence among urban teenagers. He also serves as youth pastor at the First Baptist Church in Morton, Pennsylvania.

Ellen Larson is an educator and writer with degrees in education and theology. She has served as minister of Christian education in several churches, teaching teens and children, as well as their teachers. Her experience also includes teaching in public schools. She is the author of several books for Christian education teachers, and frequently leads training seminars for volunteer teachers. Ellen and her husband live in San Diego and are the parents of two daughters.

You've Made the Right Choice!

Thanks for choosing **Custom Curriculum**! We think your choice says at least three things about you:

(1) You know your group pretty well, and want your program to fit that group like a glove;

(2) You like having options instead of being boxed in by some far-off curriculum editor;

(3) You have a small mole on your left forearm, exactly two inches above the elbow.

OK, so we were wrong about the mole. But if you like having choices that help you tailor meetings to fit your kids, **Custom Curriculum** *is* the best place to be.

Going through Customs

In this (and every) **Custom Curriculum** volume, you'll find
• five great sessions you can use anytime, in any order.
• reproducible student handouts, at least one per session.
• a truckload of options for adapting the sessions to your group (more about that in a minute).
• a helpful get-you-ready article by a youth expert.
• clip art for making posters, fliers, and other kinds of publicity to get kids to your meetings.

Each **Custom Curriculum** session has three to six steps. No matter how many steps a session has, it's designed to achieve these goals:

• *Getting together.* Using an icebreaker activity, you'll help kids be glad they came to the meeting.

• *Getting thirsty.* Why should kids care about your topic? Why should they care what the Bible has to say about it? You'll want to take a few minutes to earn their interest before you start pouring the "living water."

• *Getting the Word.* By exploring and discussing carefully selected passages, you'll find out what God has to say.

• *Getting the point.* Here's where you'll help kids make the leap from principles to nitty-gritty situations they are likely to face.

• *Getting personal.* What should each group member do as a result of this session? You'll help each person find a specific "next-step" response that works for him or her.

Each session is written to last 45 to 60 minutes. But what if you have less time—or more? No problem! **Custom Curriculum** is all about . . . options!

What Are My Options?

Every **Custom Curriculum** session gives you fourteen kinds of options:

• *Extra Action*—for groups that learn better when they're physically moving (instead of just reading, writing, and discussing).

• *Combined Junior High/High School*—to use when you're mixing age levels, and an activity or case study would be too "young" or "old" for part of the group.

• *Small Group*—for adapting activities that would be tough with groups of fewer than eight kids.

• *Large Group*—to alter steps for groups of more than twenty kids.

• *Urban*—for fitting sessions to urban facilities and multiethnic (especially African-American) concerns.

• *Heard It All Before*—for fresh approaches that get past the defenses of kids who are jaded by years in church.

• *Little Bible Background*—to use when most of your kids are strangers to the Bible, or haven't made a Christian commitment.

• *Mostly Guys*—to focus on guys' interests and to substitute activities they might be more enthused about.

• *Mostly Girls*—to address girls' concerns and to substitute activities they might prefer.

• *Extra Fun*—for longer, more "rowdy" youth meetings where the emphasis is on fun.

• *Short Meeting Time*—tips for condensing the session to 30 minutes or so.

• *Fellowship & Worship*—for building deeper relationships or enabling kids to praise God together.

• *Media*—to spice up meetings with video, music, or other popular media.

• *Sixth Grade*—appearing only in junior high/middle school volumes, this option helps you change steps that sixth graders might find hard to understand or relate to.

• *Extra Challenge*—appearing only in high school volumes, this option lets you crank up the voltage for kids who are ready for more Scripture or more demanding personal application.

Each kind of option is offered twice in each session. So in this book, you get *almost 150* ways to tweak the meetings to fit your group!

Customizing a Session

All right, you may be thinking. *With all of these options flying around, how do I put a session together? I don't have a lot of time, you know.*

We know! That's why we've made **Custom Curriculum** as easy to follow as possible. Let's take a look at how you might prepare an actual meeting. You can do that in four easy steps:

(1) *Read the basic session plan.* Start by choosing one or more of the goals listed at the beginning of the session. You have three to pick from: a goal that emphasizes *knowledge*, one that stresses *understanding*, and one that emphasizes *action*. Choose one or more, depending on what *you* want to accomplish. Then read the basic plan to see what will work for you and what might not.

(2) *Choose your options.* You don't *have* to use any options at all; the

basic session plan would work well for many groups, and you may want to stick with it if you have absolutely no time to consider options. But if you want a more perfect fit, check out your choices.

As you read the basic session plan, you'll see small symbols in the margin. Each symbol stands for a different kind of option. When you see a symbol, it means that kind of option is offered for that step. Turn to the page noted by the symbol and you'll see that option explained.

Let's say you have a small group, mostly guys who get bored if they don't keep moving. You'll want to keep an eye out for three kinds of options: Small Group, Mostly Guys, and Extra Action. As you read the basic session, you might spot symbols that tell you there are Small Group options for Step 1 and Step 3—maybe a different way to play a game so that you don't need big teams, and a way to cover several Bible passages when just a few kids are looking them up. Then you see symbols telling you that there are Mostly Guys options for Step 2 and Step 4—perhaps a substitute activity that doesn't require too much self-disclosure, and a case study guys will relate to. Finally you see symbols indicating Extra Action options for Step 2 and Step 3—maybe an active way to get kids' opinions instead of handing out a survey, and a way to act out some verses instead of just looking them up.

After reading the options, you might decide to use four of them. You base your choices on your personal tastes and the traits of your group that you think are most important right now. **Custom Curriculum** offers you more options than you'll need, so you can pick your current favorites and plug others into future meetings if you like.

(3) *Use the checklist.* Once you've picked your options, keep track of them with the simple checklist that appears at the end of each option section (just before the start of the next session plan). This little form gives you a place to write down the materials you'll need too—since they depend on the options you've chosen.

(4) *Get your stuff together.* Gather your materials; photocopy any Repro Resources (reproducible student sheets) you've decided to use. And . . . you're ready!

The Custom Curriculum Challenge

Your kids are fortunate to have you as their leader. You see them not as a bunch of generic teenagers, but as real, live, unique kids. You care whether you really connect with them. That's why you're willing to take a few extra minutes to tailor your meetings to fit.

It's a challenge to work with real, live kids, isn't it? We think you deserve a standing ovation for taking that challenge. And we pray that **Custom Curriculum** helps you shape sessions that shape lives for Jesus Christ and His kingdom.

—*The Editors*

Talking to Kids about Style

by Les Christie

Adolescent psychologist David Elkind of Tufts University has done much to help us understand why teens act and feel the way they do. Drawing from the work of Piaget, Elkind identified several characteristics of adolescent behavior.

One characteristic is what Elkind calls the "imaginary audience." Because teenagers are primarily preoccupied with themselves, they assume everyone else is preoccupied with them too. They believe that everyone in their vicinity is thinking about what they're thinking about—namely "me." Kids feel as if they are constantly onstage, surrounded by an imaginary audience.

This is why young teenagers spend so much time in the bathroom bathing or styling their hair. When a young person stands in front of a mirror, he or she imagines how other people will see him or her and what they will think. Everyone does this to some extent, but with teenagers it becomes obsessive.

One Person's Journey

As a freshman, Megan MacKenzie came into the youth group with an entirely different set of values and attitudes than the mainstream of our group. She was a "death rocker." She dressed in black, wore black mascara, and dyed her blond hair black. She hung out with kids at school who were considered misfits and rebels. She stayed by herself or with a few friends, rarely moving beyond her little clique.

Within a year, Megan's style of dress, taste in music, and way of thinking began to change. To be sure, she still maintained her own personality, but Megan had become more open, and she had developed a growing appreciation for others.

The key to her change was acceptance, not only by the adult leaders in the youth group, but also by the other members of the group. They simply loved her and allowed her to be herself. When Megan felt she fit in with the youth group, she slowly began to change in a positive way, even though she was accepted as she was.

Megan changed, but still kept much of her own style and personality. The Lord, working through the youth group, was able to sand off the rough edges of her life without destroying who Megan was. She remained the original that she was. She kept her curiosity about life, her creativity, her poetry, and her zest for learning.

Avoiding the "Cookie Cutter" Mentality

One of the dangers of this type of book is thinking there is one "cookie cutter" mold that every kid has to fit into. What *should* the kids in your group look like, be like, act like? I would hope there is room for diversity, and there are leaders and kids who have the ability to accommodate the unusual.

No two fingerprints are alike, no two snowflakes are alike, no two voice prints are alike, and no two retinas of the eye are alike. Don't rob kids of the opportunity to become the people God intends for them to be. No one else can smile their smiles. No one else has ever lived—or ever will live—who has their combination of abilities, talents, friends, burdens, sorrows, and physical attributes. If they didn't exist there would be a hole in creation, a gap in history, something missing from God's plan. Each of us is custom designed, handcrafted, and original. There is not an ordinary person in your youth group.

Back in the dark ages (the 1960s) when I began in youth ministry, there was one model that we wanted kids to be like. There was one type of music that ninety percent of the kids listened to, and only one style of clothes that was "in." Not so in today's society.

It's difficult to select a style of Christian music that will appeal to kids in our group. There is no one monolithic, clear-cut, dominant music style. At a conference I recently attended, there were three different Christian bands that played one evening for a concert. Each band featured a different style (heavy metal, rap, and pop), and each appealed to a huge group of kids.

One of our tasks as youth workers is to help our kids, with all their different tastes, to get along. This won't happen with a couple of Bible lessons over a short period of time. It takes work and patience. We need to focus on helping our kids appreciate each other.

The Beauty of Diversity

Many times, as we look at music and clothes, we emphasize outward appearance but never deal with the attitude behind the style or look. Not every kid who dresses differently or listens to a unique type of music is trying to be rebellious. Nor is every kid who looks conservative and listens to Lawrence Welk well-behaved and respectful.

The cars parked in my church's parking lot reflect this diversity in personal style. Some people drive sturdy, sedate four-door sedans. Others drive affordable family station wagons or minivans. Some drive opulent gas guzzlers that ride and steer like oceangoing yachts, and cost about the same. Some have four-wheel-drive, four-feet-off-the-ground, all-terrain vehicles. Some people drive dented, rusted, smoke-belching relics. Some people's cars have bumper stickers that say, "My other car is a Rolls." Others have bumper stickers that say, "My other car is a piece of junk too."

We all enjoy the freedom to choose our individual style. What if everyone were issued a yellow Hyundai? Within a week, people would paint the cars different colors, stretch them, and add sunroofs to make them individual, unique—theirs.

Some of your group members probably are obsessed with clothes; they may spend hours each night deciding what they're going to wear the next day. Others couldn't care less what they wear; they simply put on whatever is available. Neither style is better than the other; the two styles are just different.

Most teens, as well as many adults, have a difficult time discovering their style or defining it. So there's probably no reason to panic when kids try different styles—as long as they're not harming themselves or others. Trying on different styles is how we discover what's most comfortable and right for us. When I first started speaking, I would copy the delivery styles and message preparation of speakers I admired. Over time, I developed my own style—but it still had some of the elements of the people I admired.

What about Cliques?

Teens tend to hang around people who have similar styles in music, clothes, and attitude. Over time, cliques can develop. Eric Johnson defines a clique as "a small group of friends who stick together and shut others out." Ideally, we want to foster a feeling of unity within the group, with each person expressing openness and friendliness toward everyone else. But that's difficult to achieve. Even though teens regard cliques as unfair or wrong, they can't seem to avoid them. I've never had much success with breaking up cliques.

It is possible, however, to reduce the destructive or negative aspects of cliques. One way is to provide as many opportunities as possible for interaction and participation. Rather than lecture on the evils of cliques, it's best to involve kids in a variety of activity-centered learning experiences that require communication and cooperation with each other.

Community and friendships usually develop as a by-product of something else. If a group of kids puts on a play, goes on a long trip, or participates together in a service project, chances are good that cliques will be reduced and community building will happen.

Some kids, like Megan, may be so unique that they have a difficult time making any friends and finding acceptance from others in the group. They may be rejected because of their appearance, personality, or mannerisms. Try to help these kids fit into the total group. We should do whatever we can to find out why a person is being rejected and, whenever possible, provide help. There are no easy answers. But the sensitive youth worker will give special attention to kids who need it, and will find creative ways to discourage the natural tendency of teens to ignore people who may be a little different. Kids are much more complex and multidimensional than most people realize, so throw away the cookie cutter and enjoy your unique group.

Les Christie is a twenty-six-year veteran of youth ministry. He has been at the same church for twenty-one years. Les is a sought-after, popular national convention speaker to both youth and adults. He has authored dozens of articles and books, including Unsung Heroes *(Youth Specialties). He is married, has two children, and lives in Placentia, California.*

The images on these two pages are designed to help you promote this course within your church and community. Feel free to photocopy anything here and adapt it to fit your publicity needs. The stuff on this page could be used as a flier that you send or hand out to kids—or as a bulletin insert. The stuff on the next page could be used to add visual interest to newsletters, calendars, bulletin boards, or other promotions. Be creative and have fun!

What's Your Style?

What do your choices about your music, your clothes, and your attitude say about you—and your relationship with Jesus? We'll be looking at stuff like this in a new course called *You've Got Style!* It's a fun topic, and an important one. Come and learn in style!

Who:

When:

Where:

Questions? Call:

You've Got Style!

You've Got Style!

What's your music style?

What's your clothing style?

Image is everything . . .
Or is it?

Guaranteed to keep you awake!

What's Your Style?

YOUR GOALS FOR THIS SESSION:

Choose one or more

☐ To help kids discover that Paul encouraged Timothy to maintain a godly personal style and not conform to others.

☐ To help kids understand that they can express their individuality in God-pleasing ways.

☐ To help kids feel confident about choosing what God wants them to do and not to feel pressured to conform.

☐ Other _____
_____

Your Bible Base:

Galatians 5:16-26
1 Timothy 6:11-16, 20, 21
1 Peter 1:13-16

Slammin' Jammin' Style

(Needed: Paper, trash can, chair or table)

O P T I O N S

As group members arrive, hand each one a few sheets of wadded-up paper. Set a trash can on a chair or table. (The trash can should be at chest level for most of your group members.) Then have group members take turns slam-dunking the paper wads into the trash can. The catch is that each group member must do an *original* dunk; he or she can't copy someone else's dunking style. After each dunk, have group members vote as to whether the dunk was original or not.

Play for two or three rounds. As the dunking showcase progresses, encourage participants to become more and more creative. For instance, they might use twists, turns, or reverses. They might bounce the paper wad off the walls or ceiling. They might dunk with their eyes closed—anything to make the dunks more spectacular.

When everyone has finished, say: **Isn't it amazing how many different ways there are to get a little piece of paper into a trash can? You can do it flamboyantly, as we've just seen—or you can do it simply.** Walk over to the trash can and simply drop the paper wad in it.

The Elements of Style

(Needed: Pencils, copies of Repro Resource 1, chalkboard and chalk or newsprint and marker)

We've just seen each other's styles when it comes to dunking paper wads. In what other areas do you show your style? Make sure your group members don't get too narrowly focused in their answers. We exhibit our personal style in almost *everything* we do—the way we walk, the way we talk, the clothes we wear, the music we listen to, the books we read, the way we drive, and the way we compete.

Everyone has a style, whether it's obvious or subtle. When might a person's style be really obvious? (With friends, playing a sport, one-on-one, and so on)

When might a person's style be less obvious? (In class, with parents, in church)

Ask: **What's the connection between a person's style and the people he or she is with?** (Someone might act more like himself or herself with his or her friends than with a teacher. In the heat of competition, a person's true self might come out. On the other hand, a person's style might be very consistent no matter what type of situation he or she is in.)

Pass out copies of "The Many Styles of Kyle" (Repro Resource 1). Have group members read about one day in the life of a guy named Kyle. As they read, they should write in the margins descriptions of Kyle's style in various situations. When they've finished reading, they should go back and circle situations that sound faintly familiar, and describe *their* styles in these situations.

When everyone is finished, have several volunteers describe Kyle's style as well as their own styles in similar situations.

Then ask: **What do you think about the way Kyle expressed his style? Was it wrong? Was it OK?** If no one mentions it, point out that there are times when a person's style is morally wrong. But in Kyle's case, his style had more to do with who he was and his personal taste, rather than some big moral issue.

Explain: **Even if we all had the same set of situations with the same group of people, we would probably all make different choices because we're different people.**

Your personal style reflects your character—whether that's good, bad, or so-so. Since style is so much a part of who we are, we need to see what God has to say about it.

STEP 3

Which Way Does He Go?

(Needed: Bibles, chalkboard and chalk or newsprint and marker)

Have group members turn in their Bibles to I Timothy 6:11-16, 20, 21. As they do so, give a little background information about Timothy

and why Paul wrote this letter to him.

Timothy was a young man (I Timothy 4:12) and had been left in charge of caring for the church in Ephesus (I Timothy 1:3). Some fifteen years earlier, Timothy had met Paul when the apostle traveled through Lystra on his second missionary journey (Acts 16:1-3). Timothy had a strong faith, having been taught by his godly mother and grandmother (II Timothy 1:5), but he still needed encouragement with his responsibility. That's why Paul wrote him.

Explain: **As a young, impressionable leader of a church, Timothy had to deal with problems and conflicts. He may have felt pulled in different directions, trying to please everyone. Paul wrote him a letter, reminding him about maintaining a godly style.**

Have someone read aloud I Timothy 6:11-16. Then say: **Paul starts off with kind of a negative command to flee all this. To find out what Paul wanted Timothy to flee from, skim verses 3-10 of this same chapter.** Give group members a chance to do so.

Then ask: **Why did Paul tell Timothy to flee from the pursuit of riches? Did he have something against rich people or being rich?** (Basically, Paul wanted Timothy to flee from the attitude and lifestyle of pursuing riches and material wealth. Timothy needed to avoid the attitude some people had who thought godliness was a means to financial gain [see vs. 5]. Why? Because some people were so caught up in money, they wandered from the faith. That's why Paul said the *love* of money is a root of all kinds of evil.)

Ask group members to name the positive reminders Paul gave the young church leader. (Answers should include the following: Pursue righteousness, godliness, faith, love, endurance, and gentleness; fight the good fight; take hold of the eternal life; and keep the commands Paul had just given.)

How might these reminders help someone change his or her personal style? (For example, if you're rather cutthroat when you play basketball, you might need to work on becoming a bit more gentle. Or if you have tendency to quit when things get tough, you might need to work on endurance.)

Have someone read aloud I Timothy 6:20, 21. Then ask: **What kind of pressure do you think Timothy may have felt from other people?** (Timothy may have felt pressure to give in to the false ideas some people were pushing.)

What was Paul's advice to Timothy, and why do you think Paul gave it? (Paul advised Timothy to guard what had been entrusted to his care and to turn away from godless chatter. Timothy needed to remember that he was in charge of the care of the church—not the people spreading false doctrines. He could stand up to them, and not go along with their godless chatter and false ideas.)

Explain: **Paul didn't want Timothy to become his clone, but**

he did want Timothy to be bold and assertive about his personal style of godliness—which can be a hard thing to do.

STEP
4

Incidents Not Accidents

(Needed: Watch with a second hand, pencils, copies of Repro Resource 2)

Pass out copies of "Choose It or Lose It" (Repro Resource 2). Explain: **After I read aloud each situation, you will have ten seconds to circle your response. Don't spend a lot of time thinking about what answer to choose, just go with your first reaction.**

Make sure you keep track of time after you read each situation. When ten seconds are up, call "Time," and move on to the next situation.

When you're finished, go back through the situations, and have group members share their responses.

Ask: **Based on your quick responses, what conclusions can you make about your personal style? Think of a phrase to describe your style.** Phrases might include "To avoid is to survive" (to describe a style that avoids confrontation) or "There's safety in numbers" (to describe a conforming type of style).

Say: **No matter what sort of situations we're in, whether humorous or serious, we can make choices that reflect a personal style of godliness.**

Have group members form teams of three or four. Instruct each team to read I Peter 1:13-16 and Galatians 5:22-26, and come up with a list of the basics of a godly lifestyle.

Give the teams a few minutes to work; then have them share their answers. Their responses will probably include the following: love, joy, peace, patience, kindness, goodness, faithfulness, self-control, holiness, and not conforming to evil.

Take a few minutes to contrast this list with the acts of the sinful nature in Galatians 5:19-21.

Then ask: **What's the relationship between a person's personal style and a godly lifestyle?** (Even though a godly lifestyle has more to do with a person's character than his or her actions, it does influence the choices a person makes and the way he or she treats other people.)

Explain: **Instead of giving us a list of things to avoid, God gives us lists about character traits He wants to develop in us. It might make things a little harder, but in the long run it helps us to discover our own styles.**

Style: The First Frontier

(Needed: Small notebook for each group member [optional])

Before this session, you might want to buy small, inexpensive notebooks for your group members to use as journals.

Explain: **Most of us don't even think about our style of doing things. But this week, try to catch yourself acting a certain way, saying certain things, or being with certain people.** If you bought notebooks for your group, hand these out now. Encourage group members to keep track of these things in their journals, focusing on things that are unique to their own style and are God-honoring.

Say: **As you go about your week, remember that God has given each of us an individual style. No two people are alike, and shouldn't try to be identical.**

In the next few weeks, we're going to talk about the different things that make up style—such as the music you listen to, your look, your attitudes, and the way you get along with other people and their styles.

Close in prayer, thanking God that He's made us all unique with our own styles. Ask God to help your group members be bold and strong in expressing their personal styles of godliness.

THE MANY STYLES OF KYLE

Every morning when Kyle gets out of bed, he stumbles into the bathroom. He rubs his face several times to wake himself up. He brushes his teeth, forgetting to put the cap back on the toothpaste—as usual. At the breakfast table, Kyle inhales his cereal while reading the back of the cereal box and watching TV at the same time.

On the bus to school, Kyle makes sure that he talks to everyone worth talking to, especially the girl he has been trying to get a date with since last year. And when the bus hits a huge pothole, Kyle manages to jump the highest in his seat just to get the biggest laugh.

In math class, Kyle starts off listening intently to Mrs. Turner, but decides to finish his essay on democracy for English class when Mrs. Turner gives the class time to work on the next day's algebra assignment. He also puts some finishing touches on his ultimate love letter to the girl on the bus.

At lunch Kyle wolfs down his burrito so that he can entirely rewrite his English essay because he found out the assignment was on 19th Century English authors. Kyle is totally unaware that he also tossed out his love letter with his trash.

Later, in gym class, Kyle takes out his frustrations by playing a powerhouse game of volleyball. He's all over the place! Spiking, serving, diving, winning!

When school is over, Kyle rushes out of the building, not wanting to hang around and talk.

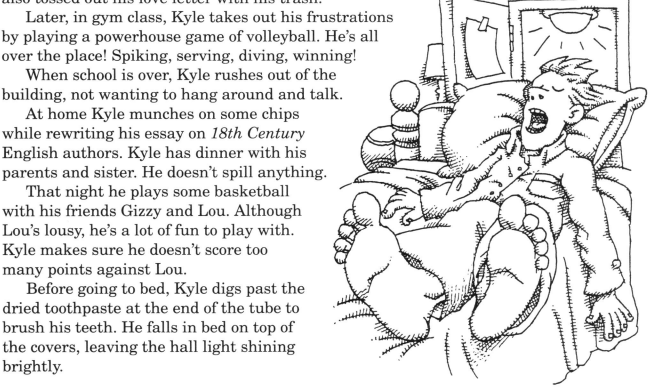

At home Kyle munches on some chips while rewriting his essay on *18th Century* English authors. Kyle has dinner with his parents and sister. He doesn't spill anything.

That night he plays some basketball with his friends Gizzy and Lou. Although Lou's lousy, he's a lot of fun to play with. Kyle makes sure he doesn't score too many points against Lou.

Before going to bed, Kyle digs past the dried toothpaste at the end of the tube to brush his teeth. He falls in bed on top of the covers, leaving the hall light shining brightly.

Choose It or Lose It

1. There's a new kid in history class. She's kind of quiet and wears last year's clothes. When class is over you
   - (a) leave as quickly as you usually do—ready for lunch.
   - (b) yell out, "Hey, I got some clothes you can rent, real cheap too!"
   - (c) go over, introduce yourself, and say, "See you tomorrow."
   - (d) other _____

2. You're at the mall with a bunch of your friends. Everyone heads to a cool clothing store to look at the jeans. One by one, each person chooses a pair and goes over to the register. As the cashier starts punching in the prices, you
   - (a) grab a pair yourself, and fall in line.
   - (b) grab two pairs, a belt, and a sweatshirt, and fall in line.
   - (c) say "I'll be right back," and head for the music store to buy the new CD you really want—and can afford.
   - (d) other _____

3. The whole family is together at Uncle Frank's. You've just had dessert when you're cousin Tanya tells you that Aunt Mildred is looking for you. Aunt Mildred wants to see how much you've grown. You
   - (a) hide in a broom closet.
   - (b) tell Tanya to tell Aunt Mildred that you've joined the Marines and are leaving right now.
   - (c) smile and go over to Aunt Mildred, enduring all of her cheek pinching.
   - (d) other _____

4. After school, your friend Alex tells you that someone has been spreading lies about him. After hearing the whole story, you
   - (a) say, "Boy, that's a shame" and change the subject.
   - (b) start thinking up a nasty rumor to spread about the person who lied about Alex.
   - (c) sympathize with him, but help him to put things in perspective.
   - (d) other _____

5. It's Saturday afternoon and you're about ready to flip on the TV, when your dad asks for some help in cleaning up the yard. You
   - (a) fake a pulled muscle and hobble over to a chair, breathing painfully.
   - (b) complain like there's no tomorrow, do very little to help, and actually make the job a lot worse than it really was.
   - (c) grab your Walkman and help out, knowing that the sooner the work is over, the sooner you can turn on the TV.
   - (d) other _____

EXTRA ACTION

Step 2
Have kids stand at arm's length from each other, facing the front of the room. Read the story of Kyle aloud from Repro Resource 1. Pause briefly after reading each of Kyle's actions so that kids can act out what *they* might do in a similar situation. For example, instead of stumbling to the bathroom in the morning, they might be wide awake and smiling. Instead of taking out their frustrations by playing volleyball, they might listen to music or even scream. Discuss some of your group members' reactions. Which are right? Which are wrong? Which are neither?

Step 3
Add action to the Bible study with the following activity. Have two teams read I Timothy 6:3-16. One team will look for things to flee, the other for things to pursue. Each team will write its discoveries on sheets of 8 1/2" x 11" poster board, one answer per sheet. Mix up the sheets. Then tape them on the floor, writing side up, with masking tape or duct tape as if they were spaces on a game board. Kids must walk the path as quickly as possible, stepping only on "pursue" qualities and avoiding "flee" traits. Anyone who falls off the path is out. Keep increasing the pace until you're down to just a few kids, who are the winners. In Step 4, skip the Repro Resource. Read the Galatians 5:22-26 qualities out loud and have kids strike "statue" poses for each. As kids hold each pose, ask: **Does that feel comfortable or not? If it doesn't feel comfortable, is that because this quality isn't part of your style? What can you do about that?**

SMALL GROUP

Step I
Hard to get your few kids "pumped" for slam-dunking? Try the following activity instead. Bring some crayon drawings done by young children. (If you don't have young kids at home, maybe a Sunday school teacher can get you some drawings.) Don't let your group members see the pictures yet. Pass out paper (the kind used for the drawings you brought) and crayons. Have group members sit as far apart from each other as possible while they draw pictures as young children might. Let them know that their "forgeries" will be competing against the real thing. Then mix their drawings up with the real children's artwork and display all the drawings together. See whether kids can guess which are real children's drawings and which are imitations. Give a prize for the "best fake." Use this activity to illustrate how hard it can be to imitate someone else's style—and how unnecessary it is when our own style is just fine.

Step 5
Take advantage of your group's size with a more personal application. Have group members form pairs. Give each pair a paper grocery bag that you've just soaked with water. At your signal, each pair will stuff crumpled newspaper into its bag. See which pair can pack in the most pages without tearing its bag. After congratulating the winners, ask: **Where and when do you most feel like your style doesn't fit? Is there something wrong with your style—or with the "bag" you're trying to fit into?** After discussing this, ask partners to phone each other once during the week to say something like, "No matter how much you're pressured to fit in, I hope you'll still be yourself."

LARGE GROUP

Step I
If the slam-dunk contest would result in a long line of waiting kids with nothing to do, and reading the Repro Resource in Step 2 wouldn't hold the group's attention, try the following activity. Replace Steps I and 2 with a more involving opener. Assign kids randomly to six teams. Each team will sit in its own circle and start with the following identities and conversation topics: (1) jocks, talking about football; (2) metalheads, discussing why metal music is so great; (3) computer brains, arguing over which is better, IBM or Apple; (4) rich kids, discussing the country clubs their parents belong to; (5) dropouts, complaining about the fast-food places where they work; (6) mall rats, rating clothing stores and video arcades. Every 90 seconds, at your signal, each team must get up and switch places with another team, taking on the other team's identity and topic of conversation. Do this until all teams have had a chance to "try on" all the identities. Ask for a show of hands to see which styles kids felt most and least comfortable with. Discuss: **Are some of these styles wrong and others right? Or are they just different? Why?** Rejoin the basic session plan at the last paragraph in Step 2.

Step 4
Sharing Repro Resource responses and describing personal styles might take too long. Try skipping the Repro Resource. Have kids form ten "cliques"—one for each quality found in the I Peter and Galatians passages. Each clique should come up with a description of what its members might wear, music they might listen to, what they'd do at the mall, what movies they'd go to, and how they'd treat other cliques. Let a spokesperson for each clique share results as time allows.

HEARD IT ALL BEFORE

Step 3

Jaded kids may think they know exactly what style the Bible wants them to have: boring. Before getting into the study, acknowledge stereotypes of "Christian style." Have a prepared student volunteer come to the front of the room. Pretend to "remove" his or her personality with a scientific-looking gadget (perhaps a Dustbuster covered with tinfoil). Congratulate him or her on now having a "Christian personality." He or she should answer in a robot-like monotone a few questions about his or her new, boring style. Then let kids discuss the assumptions people make about how Christians are supposed to act. Instead of studying I Timothy, plan to use the passages listed under the "Little Bible Background," "Short Meeting Time," or "Combined Junior High/High School" options for Step 3.

Step 4

Since the "fruit of the Spirit" passage has been applied to so many subjects, you may need to approach it in a slightly different way. Skip the Repro Resource. Have group members form three teams. Each team will look at Galatians 5:19-21 (acts of the sinful nature) first. Team 1 will act out what it might be like to work in a fast-food place with a worker whose style is based on the passage. Team 2 will act out what it might be like to spend an afternoon at the mall (or hanging out on the street) with a friend who gets his or her style from the passage. Team 3 will act out a youth meeting made up of kids who get their styles from the passage. (Ask kids to leave the parts about sexual immorality and orgies to the imagination.) *Then* read and discuss Galatians 5:22-26 as a contrast.

LITTLE BIBLE BACKGROUND

Step 3

In place of the I Timothy passage, study the styles of some Bible people that kids may have heard of. Ask: **What's one thing you've heard about each of these men: Moses, David, Paul, and John the Baptist? Have you heard anything about their personalities?** Have group members form four teams. Team 1 will look at the "shy" style of Moses (Exodus 4:10-16). Team 2 will look at the physical (yet musical) David (I Samuel 16:18-23; 17:32-37). Team 3 will read about the scholarly, sometimes sarcastic Paul (Galatians 1:13, 14; 3:1-5). Team 4 will look at John the Baptist, a nonconformist (Matthew 3:1-8). Summarize what each of these people did for God (Moses liberated a nation of slaves. David served as king of Israel and wrote many of the Psalms. Paul brought the Good News about Jesus to non-Jews and wrote much of the New Testament. John the Baptist prepared the way for Jesus.) Ask: **Which of these people do you identify with most? Least? Why? How could each person's style have gotten in the way of serving God? How might each style have helped accomplish God's goals? What kind of person do you usually think of as one God can use? Does reading about these people change your mind? Why or why not?**

Step 4

You may want to explain the following terms from the passages. *Holy*—pure, blameless, set aside for a certain purpose. *Debauchery*—an out-of-control quest to satisfy wrong sexual and other desires. *Witchcraft*—literally means *medication* here; refers to magic, sorcery (casting spells, etc.). *Discord*—quarreling, fighting. *Dissensions*—lack of unity, division.

FELLOWSHIP & WORSHIP

Step 1

Help group members get to know each other with the following opener. As kids enter, give each an index card and a pen. Each person should write the following verse (in longhand if possible) on the card: "Whatever your hand finds to do, do it with all your might" (Ecclesiastes 9:10a). Collect and mix up the cards. Pass them out again, making sure no one gets his or her own. Each person should make some guesses about the person whose card he or she got, based only on the handwriting. Is it a girl? A guy? Is the person shy? Outgoing? Artistic? Into sports? What kind of music might the person like? Then have kids find the people who match the cards. When a cardholder finds a writer, the cardholder should reveal his or her guesses and find out whether any of them were right. Use this as an illustration of the assumptions we make about people based on the smallest hints about their styles.

Step 5

Have group members form four worship teams. Each team will find a short passage about God from Job or Psalms and interpret it in a distinctive way. One team should use creative movement; one should use music (using only objects found around your meeting place); one should use sound effects (made only with team members' mouths); and one should come up with its own idea of what to do. After teams share what they came up with, close with sentence prayers. Encourage kids to praise God by talking to Him in their own style—not worrying about whether their prayers sound impressive or even sound like prayers.

MOSTLY GIRLS

Step 2
Change "The Many Styles of Kyle" (Repro Resource 1) to "The Many Styles of Karol." Ask the group members to change the pronoun "he" to "she" as they read and make the appropriate changes about the love letter and date attempts on the bus. Or, if you prefer, give two or three girls copies of the resource ahead of time and ask them to change parts of it to describe themselves or girls they know. Then ask each girl to read her description. Follow this with a discussion using the questions for the original skit.

Step 3
During the discussion about Paul and Timothy, ask: **Do you think girls are more conforming to a certain "style" than guys are? Why or why not? How difficult is it for you to change your style to the biblical standards named by Paul? What if you were the only one behaving this way in your circle of friends?**

MOSTLY GUYS

Step 3
Give each person a pencil and paper. Kids should number their papers from 1 to 10. Read the following names aloud (or substitute others) and have kids write them down: **Axl Rose, Billy Graham, Tom Cruise, Mister Rogers, Ice-T, Steve Martin, William Shakespeare, Michael Jordan, Garth Brooks, Jesus Christ.** Ask: **What percentage of your own style is like that of each of these men? In other words, are you fifteen percent Ice-T, seventy percent Michael Jordan, ten percent Mister Rogers, and five percent Steve Martin?** Give guys time to work out their own percentages, which must total one hundred percent. Have them share their results. Ask: **How did you feel about including Jesus on your list? Why? Is His style "manly" or not?** Then study 1 Timothy 1:3-16. In Step 4, skip the Repro Resource and the 1 Peter passage. When you read Galatians 5:22-26, have guys come up with ways in which an action hero (Arnold Schwarzenegger, Bruce Willis, etc.) could show these qualities in a movie.

Step 5
Most guys probably won't be interested in keeping a "style journal." Instead, wrap up by affirming that there are different "guy styles." Have group members form two teams. One team will do all the push-ups it can in one minute; the other will name all the adverbs it can in one minute. Give a prize to the team that racks up the largest number of push-ups or adverbs. Ask: **Do most people you know think that guys should be able to do push-ups, name adverbs, or both? Why?** Affirm that "manliness" shouldn't be measured by push-ups *or* adverbs—or rate of physical development, interest in dating, love of sports, interest in cars, aptitude for business, or any other standard except the example of Christ. Encourage guys to use Christ—not other guys—as their role model.

EXTRA FUN

Step 1
Stage a "personality transplant." Put two chairs at the front of the room. Bring two kitchen colanders (large spaghetti-draining bowls punched with holes) onto which you've wired some scientific-looking stuff (magnetic compass, springs, plastic tubing, etc.). To start the meeting, get two volunteers to sit in the chairs while they wear the "personality transference correlators" (the colanders). Explain that you're going to switch the personalities of the two kids. Throw a switch (real or imaginary) as a helper flashes the room lights on and off. Each volunteer must then answer a series of questions (about favorite musical group, least favorite food, biggest worry, etc.) as if he or she were the other volunteer. Write down answers. Then check with the correct volunteers to find out how many answers were right. The volunteer with more right answers wins. If you have time, try it again with other pairs. Tie this into the fact that our styles are unique, not interchangeable.

Step 5
Try a "charm course relay." Have group members form two teams. While walking to the other side of the room and back each team member must (1) balance a hymnbook on his or her head; (2) say, "In church, the people stay mainly on the steeple" at least five times; and (3) keep his or her hands in a "praying hands" position (except when picking up a fallen hymnbook). Anyone dropping a hymnbook must restart from the point at which the book fell. After rewarding the winning team, ask: **If you took a "Christian charm course," do you think you'd learn skills like balancing hymnbooks on your head? What might you learn? Do you think there's such a thing as "Christian charm," a style of acting or talking or dressing that all Christians should have? Why or why not?**

Step 2

Try one of the following activities:
(1) Preview and show a couple of scenes from a movie on video that features a group of characters with contrasting styles—such as *Dead Poets Society*, *The Breakfast Club*, *Stand by Me*, or *The Goonies*. Ask: **What word describes the style of each character you saw? Did you identify with any of the characters? Why of why not? How are the styles of real-life people different from those seen in most movies and TV shows?** (2) Have a contest in which several kids compete to eat an ear of corn most quickly. Videotape the contest, being sure to zoom in and record each person's technique. After giving the winner a prize, play back the tape. Analyze the participants' styles (one row at a time, one end at a time, etc.). Use this to lead into a discussion of group members' styles in other areas—music, relating to people, attitude, clothes, etc.

Step 5

Play one or two recorded songs about personal style, many of which go beyond simply affirming one's uniqueness. If you can't find current examples, here are some oldies you might use: "The Greatest Love" (Whitney Houston); "Goodbye, Yellow Brick Road" (Elton John); "My Way" (Elvis Presley or Frank Sinatra); "I've Got to Be Me" (Sammy Davis, Jr.); "I Am, I Said" (Neil Diamond). Discuss how far we can take our personal styles before they turn into selfishness. Compare the messages of the songs with Mark 12:31.

Step 1

Combine Steps 1 and 2 in this shorter opener. Read the following situations aloud. Ask kids to show how much stress they'd feel in each situation by waving both arms (high stress), waving one arm (some stress), or pretending to fall asleep (little stress). The situations are as follows: **(1) You're trapped in an elevator with a gun collector. (2) You're trapped in an elevator with a major soap opera fan. (3) You're accepted by only one college: Clown College. (4) On the spur of the moment at a family reunion, your uncle asks you to sing "Heavenly Sunshine" like you did when you were five. (5) Halfway through your math homework, your calculator breaks. (6) Your parents forbid you to listen to heavy metal music. (7) You have to walk on crutches for three weeks. (8) Your hair dryer quits.** Ask a few volunteers to explain their answers—and what their answers may say about their styles.

Step 3

Replace Steps 3 and 4 with the following study. Read Matthew 11:16-19. Ask: **What does this tell you about Jesus' style? About trying to fit in with other people's styles?** Read 1 Corinthians 10:31–11:1. Ask: **Does this mean *any* style is OK? Why or why not? How might your style have to change around certain people to attract them to Christ?** Have teams read these sections from James 1: verses 5-8, 9-11, 13-15, 19-21, 26, 27. Ask: **What does James tell those with these styles: indecisive; "nothing but the best"; "I just can't say no"; quick-tempered; very "religious"?** Skip Step 5. Have kids consider which parts of their styles might be strengths and which might be weaknesses. Ask them to pray that God will show them how to use strengths for Him and how to deal with the weaknesses.

Step 2

Ask for two volunteers (preferably kids who like to dress stylishly) to participate in an activity. Give each one a set of "goofy" clothing—which might include items such as an ugly dress, high-water pants, a weird hat, gloves with fingers missing, mismatched socks, and "fish head" tennis shoes. Assign each volunteer a room in which to put on the clothes. Give the volunteers five minutes to make the clothing look as stylish as possible on them. They must wear every item given to them. When the volunteers are dressed, have them model their fashions for the rest of the group. Then have the group vote on which one was more stylish. Afterward, discuss the uniqueness of individual style.

Step 4

To emphasize the determination needed to live a godly lifestyle, get two volunteers who are quick thinkers capable of playing "The Dozens" (an urban youth culture game played to test how well one will stand up to insults hurled at him or her). Have them play "The Godly Dozens." One teen will be the insultee, the other the insulter. The insulter will insult or crack jokes about the character of the insultee. (But don't let it get brutal.) The task of the insultee is to respond to each insult with an appropriate *positive* statement about the character of the insulter. (For example: Insulter—"You're so little, ants call you shorty." Insultee—"You're so smart those same ants want to make you their king (or queen)." The test is to see how godly the insultee can remain.

Step 2

Want kids to think about their own styles? Studying the actions of "Kyle" may be a confusing detour. Try a simpler multiple-choice, read-aloud quiz, asking whether kids would be more like Indiana Jones, Roseanne Arnold, Mr. Spock, or Barney Fife in these situations: **(1) Somebody cuts in front of you in line at a movie. (2) It's testimony time at church. (3) You have a choice of going on a three-mile hike, baking a cake, watching TV, or reading a book. (4) A teacher unjustly accuses you of copying answers from someone else's algebra test. (5) You get to buy a whole new wardrobe. (6) You're new at school.** Let kids write down their answers. Then discuss the responses as a group if the kids are willing.

Step 3

Replace the I Timothy study with a down-to-earth look at the styles of Jesus' followers. Read about Peter (Matthew 26:31-35, 69-75; John 18:4-11; 21:4-7). Ask: **How would you describe Peter's style? Would you want a guy like him to follow you around for three years? How could Jesus use someone with Peter's style? How might He use *your* style?** Then read about Mary and Martha (Luke 10:38-42; John 11:1-6, 17-29). Ask: **How were the styles of Mary and Martha different? Did Jesus mean that Martha should always be like Mary? How did Jesus feel about Mary and Martha? Based on this, would you say Jesus wants us all to have the same style?** In Step 4, help kids understand the I Peter and Galatians qualities by asking how they might apply to the way kids answered in Step 2 under this option. In Step 5, skip the journaling idea. Wrap up with a mini-party celebrating kids' varying styles. Let them customize refreshments in their own way—perhaps choosing toppings for small pizzas or sundaes.

Step 1

If your group would like something more cerebral than slammin' and jammin', try the following activity. Write the word *style* on the board. Have group members form teams of two or three. Give each team pencils and paper. Say: **What other words can you make from the word *style*? You don't have to use all the letters. The first team to get three words wins.** It shouldn't take long for a team to get three. (Some possibilities are yes, let, set, lets, sty, and lye.) Say to the first team to get three words: **Oh, I'm sorry. You have to get the *right* three words—the *best* three.** When there are protests and questions about which words are best, just say: **If you don't know, I can't tell you.** After kids continue to protest, or to give "wrong" answers, say: **I can see some of you don't think this is fair. But don't some people treat the subject of style this way?** Have kids come up with some areas in which people's styles differ (tastes in music, personality, way of walking, etc.). Ask: **What style is the "right" one?**

Step 4

Kids may be tempted to pick the "c" answers on the Repro Resource 2 because they sound like the "Christian" ones—thereby short-circuiting the self-evaluation process. Instead of passing out the sheets, read aloud just the sentence starters (the part ending with "you" and preceding the multiple choices). Let kids finish the sentences on paper. Encourage them to write the first sentence completions that come to mind. Have them share their responses if they're willing; use these to get a handle on personal style.

Date Used:

Approx. Time

Step 1: Slammin' Jammin' Style _____
- o Small Group
- o Large Group
- o Fellowship & Worship
- o Extra Fun
- o Short Meeting Time
- o Extra Challenge
- Things needed:

Step 2: The Elements of Style _____
- o Extra Action
- o Mostly Girls
- o Media
- o Urban
- o Combined Junior High/High School
- Things needed:

Step 3: Which Way . . . _____
- o Extra Action
- o Heard It All Before
- o Little Bible Background
- o Mostly Girls
- o Mostly Guys
- o Short Meeting Time
- o Combined Junior High/High School
- Things needed:

Step 4: Incidents Not Accidents _____
- o Large Group
- o Heard It All Before
- o Little Bible Background
- o Urban
- o Extra Challenge
- Things needed:

Step 5: Style: The First Frontier _____
- o Small Group
- o Fellowship & Worship
- o Mostly Guys
- o Extra Fun
- o Media
- Things needed:

SESSION 2

Your Kind of Music

YOUR GOALS FOR THIS SESSION:

Choose one or more

☐ To help kids discover how Solomon was influenced by his wives to worship false gods and turn his back on the one true God.

☐ To help kids understand that music can have an influence on them.

☐ To help kids decide for themselves what music they should listen to, and why.

☐ Other _____
_____

Your Bible Base:

1 Kings 4:29-34; 11:1-13
Psalm 95:1-7
Philippians 4:8, 9

Let's Do Lunch

(Needed: Tape player, cassette, sunglasses, telephone, pencils, copies of Repro Resource 3)

As group members arrive, have a cassette playing some kind of music. Put on some sunglasses, and play the part of a high-powered music agent. Pick up a telephone and say things like "Sure, the deal's almost finished," "Did you hear that new band?" "Let's do lunch, we can talk about it then," "Yep, sign them to a million-dollar contract."

Hang up the phone and say: **OK, people, Mr. Wainsworth wants to make his record company the biggest music company in the Western Hemisphere! You're all part of the creative team that he wants to come up with the hottest, the coolest, the warmest new sound the world's heard since Beethoven.**

We want to stun the world! We want to sell more CDs, more tapes, more eight-tracks than anyone else ever has or ever will sell, and this group has got to do it! We want every household from Alaska to Uruguay to be playing this music. We want people to know this music backwards and forwards. It's got to be good!

Pass out copies of "Anatomy of a Band" (Repro Resource 3) and pencils. Have group members pair up to complete the sheet, filling in the descriptions of the band they want to create.

Say: **When you've finished coming up with the perfect band, I want you to pitch your band to me. I want you to sell me on your sound. Convince me to sign up your band on the spot.**

Have the pairs take turns pitching their bands to you. Encourage group members to give you a high-pressured sell, perhaps demonstrating the bands' sound and look. As the members of each pair talk, act as if you're thinking hard about their presentation—scribble notes, and promise them that you'll get back to them ("My people will talk with your people").

When the presentations are over, turn off the music. Whether or not you take off the sunglasses is up to you.

What's with Music?

(Needed: Chalkboard and chalk or newsprint and marker)

Explain: **As you created your band, you had to evaluate the different elements that go into making music. See if you can use that same kind of thinking in determining the different types of music you like.** Ask several volunteers to name some of their favorite songs and bands, and explain why those songs and bands appeal to them. If you're not familiar with a song or band that's named, ask the person to describe what it's like.

Then ask: **Why do you like the music you do?** Encourage group members to be as specific as possible with their answers. Is the music complicated? Rhythmic? Repetitious? Synthesized? Traditional? Vocal-focused? Music-focused? List some of their answers on the board.

Then ask: **Is there a type of music that you never thought you'd enjoy, but do?** If possible, talk about how your music interests have changed over the years.

What about going to concerts? Why do you go to see certain groups? Have you ever gone to see a group that was totally new to you? Give group members a few minutes to talk about their concert-going experiences, Christian or otherwise.

Then say: **Music can be a powerful thing. It can raise money for farmers or rally a country together around a flag. It can even bring back memories.** Encourage several group members to talk about songs that bring back memories for them of a particular time, place, and person.

How does the music we listen to influence our style? (If you think the members of a certain group are cool, you might want to copy their look. You might begin to support the causes they support and live the lifestyle they endorse.)

STEP 3

Under the Influence

(Needed: Bibles)

Say: **Let's take a break from music for a moment, and let's just consider the influence people and other things can have on us.**

Have group members turn to I Kings 4. As they do, give them a little background about King Solomon. He was made king over Israel by his father, David (I Kings 1:32-35). He married the daughter of Pharaoh and brought her to Jerusalem (I Kings 3:1). God told Solomon to ask for whatever he wanted, and Solomon pleased God by asking for wisdom. God gave Solomon wisdom, along with riches and honor (I Kings 3:5-13). God promised Solomon a long life if he were obedient like David (I Kings 3:14).

Have someone read aloud I Kings 4:29-34. Then say: **Solomon seems to have it made. He sounds like a great guy. He loved music. He knew about nature—and about almost everything else, it seems. Not only that, he also owned a massive fortune. He had twenty-five tons of gold, and everyone who came to visit him—which was the whole world according to I Kings 10:24—brought him a gift.**

However, the story doesn't end there. Read on. Have group members turn to I Kings 11:1-13. Ask a couple volunteers to take turns reading the passage aloud.

Then say: **Describe the influence Solomon's wives had on him.** (His foreign wives influenced Solomon to worship their false gods and idols. This steady influence of sin in Solomon's life slowly, over time, drew him away from obedience to God.)

What went wrong and why? (Solomon ignored the Lord's warning about marrying foreign women who worshiped false gods and idols, and he ended up turning his heart to these gods. He no longer followed the Lord completely and did evil in the eyes of the Lord.)

What do you think Solomon could have done to change this downhill slide? (As king, Solomon could have destroyed the idols and abolished idol worship. With all his wisdom, Solomon probably had the guts to stand up to his wives—and he should have. Solomon should have confessed his sin and turned back to God.)

Summarize: **Solomon's life can be divided into two parts. At first, he was influenced by wisdom and obedience, and the** result was honor and wealth. But then he was influenced by his many wives to worship idols, and the result was enemy invasions and rebellion in his own kingdom.

STEP
4

An Influential Tune

(Needed: Chalkboard and chalk or newsprint and marker)

Who or what has an influence on you? Have group members call out answers, and keep track of their responses on the board. Possible answers might include friends, TV, movies, parents, brothers, sisters, teachers, and music.

Then ask: **How would you rank these, from the most influential to the least?** Encourage group members to talk with each other, and come up with a unanimous decision about the ranking. Number the items on the board accordingly.

Then say: **Let's get back to music. It's on our list.** (If it's not, add it to the list.) **Why did you give it this ranking?** Since the ranking was a group decision, ask individuals if they wanted to give music a higher or lower ranking than the rest of the group did.

Say: **The music industry loves you! They target young adults in magazines, on television, and on radio. Christian music is the same way. Music is big business and they want your business.**

But how can you tell if a band is going to have a negative or positive affect on you? Encourage group members to explain how they choose a CD or tape to listen to or buy. If some group members say that they only listen to Christian music, ask them to explain why.

Then ask: **If the members of a band are Christians, does that automatically make their music good? Why or why not?** (Not necessarily. There's a lot of faulty theology in some Christian music.)

What sort of buyer's guidelines do you think God has about listening to music? Get a few responses.

Then have someone read aloud Philippians 4:8, 9. As the person is reading, write the following words on the board: true, noble, right, pure, lovely, admirable, excellent, and praiseworthy.

Ask: **Is this passage saying that we have to examine every single word of every single song to see if it's true, noble,**

OPTIONS

HEARD IT ALL BEFORE

LITTLE BIBLE BACKGROUND

MOSTLY GIRLS

MOSTLY GUYS

MEDIA

SHORT MEETING TIME

URBAN

right, pure, lovely, admirable, excellent, and praiseworthy?
Group members probably will agree that the idea is pretty extreme

Actually, these are things that you're supposed to think about, which makes the real question trickier to answer.

Does the music you listen to make it easier or harder for you to think about the qualities listed in Philippians 4:8, 9?
Have group members seriously consider the music they listen to. Is it true? Noble? Right? Pure? Lovely? Admirable? Excellent? Praiseworthy? Don't ask anyone to answer out loud.

Point out that a person's thoughts eventually influence his or her actions. So, if you think about things that are true, noble, pure, and excellent, you will start living a life of moral excellence. Unfortunately, the converse is true as well.

Say: **Think about a gold miner using a mining pan to sift through the sand and gravel at the bottom of a stream. He uses the pan to sift out the gold. Likewise, God has given us a filter right here in these two verses through which we can pour the things that influence our lives.**

STEP
5

Check That Dial

(Needed: Bibles, paper, markers)

You can start using God's filter by taking stock of your personal music collection. Think about your answers to these questions:

What stations do you have preset on your stereo?

How often do you listen to music? Is it too much or too little?

What kind of music dominates your collection?

Do you need more variety, less variety, or is it fine the way it is?

Based on your answers, think of a way to describe your style when it comes to music. Encourage several group members to explain their descriptions.

Afterward, have them turn to Psalm 95:1-7. Read the passage aloud together as a group. Encourage group members to memorize verses 1 and 2.

If your group members are comfortable doing so, have them pray aloud about the music they choose to listen to. If they're not comfortable, have them pray silently. After a few minutes, pray aloud, asking God to strengthen your group members in examining the things that influence their lives.

ANATOMY
OF A
B A N D

Describe the NAME of the band.
• Is the name spelled like it sounds,
or does it have an odd spelling
(like Led Zeppelin and Def Leppard)?
• What significance does the name have?

Describe the PEOPLE in the band.
• How many band members are there?
• How many of them are guys? How many of them are girls?
• How old are they?
• What do they look like?
• What kind of clothes or outfits do they wear onstage?
• What are their concerts like? What do they do onstage?
• What is it about them that separates them from the members of other bands?

Describe the MUSIC of the band.
• Is it dance music? Country? Blues? Folk? Rock? Alternative? Pop? Rap? Metal?
A combination of one or more of these?
• Is the music generally fast or slow? Is it loud or mellow?
• What are the primary instruments? Drums? Guitars? Electonic keyboards? Bass? Piano?
• Is there anything unusual about the band's sound? Do they use any odd instruments like
an accordion or a xylophone?
• What are the vocals like? Who or what does the singer sound like?

Describe the LYRICS of the band.
• How hard is it to understand what's being sung?
• Do the lyrics rhyme, for the most part? Are they repetitious?
• Are they personal? Are they cryptic?
• Do they focus mainly on love and relationship issues? Do they focus on political and
social issues?
• Are the lyrics controversial?

Step 1

Have kids make paper "dolls" of their own design—leaving off the legs. Instruct the kids to tape the dolls to the backs of their hands and use their index and middle fingers as the dolls' legs. Line kids up along one side of a table for a "dance contest." Turn on a radio and tune it to various music stations, about ten seconds per station, while kids let their fingers do the dancing with each type of music. Give prizes for most energetic dancing, most original, etc. Then discuss what music moves us to do, the influence it can have over us.

Step 2

Supply paper and markers. Have each group member indicate his or her favorite music by designing a "world tour" T-shirt for his or her favorite artist or group. For Step 3, bring several rolls of masking tape. Let one of your guys demonstrate how easily he can tear a piece of tape. Then have him sit on a "throne" at the front while the group reads I Kings 4:29-34. Give the rolls of tape to your group members. Each time a question is asked and answered about I Kings 11:1-13, kids will tape the "king" more securely to his throne. At the end of the step, the king will try to get loose. Use this to illustrate how Solomon was gradually trapped by the influence of his wives. In Step 4, after ranking influences, choose five kids to answer the remaining discussion questions. Each answerer will come to the front of the room and put on headphones (connected to a personal stereo that's playing loud rock). The person must listen to your question and answer it with the headphones on. At the end of the step, ask: **What kind of "influence" did the music in the headphones have? How is that like the way music can affect us?**

Step 1

The band-creating project may be hard to do with just a few kids. If that's the case for you, try the following activity. Bring several recorded songs of various styles; the exact number and style don't matter. Play about half a minute of each song. After each selection, have volunteers complete these sentences: **(1) That song made me feel . . . (2) That song would be better if it were recorded by . . . (3) If I had to listen to that song every day, I'd . . . (4) A song I like better than that one is . . .** Use this to lead into the Step 2 discussion of the music kids like most.

Step 5

Make the most of your group's size with a more interactive wrap-up. Instead of reading Psalm 95:1-7, have kids look in hymnbooks for a hymn whose message the whole group thinks is pretty good. Then have each person answer this question for the rest of the group: **How might you change this song—lyrics, music, and the instruments with which it's usually played—to fit your style?** After hearing replies, encourage kids to come up with new church music in the future that fits their styles, and to learn to appreciate the styles of others.

Step 1

Most of your group could get restless while pairs "pitch" bands to you. An involving alternative would be to have an impromptu musical, *A Guy Named Bob*. Have group members form five "choruses." Chorus A will choose a familiar children's song to sing. Chorus B will choose a love song. Chorus C will choose a sad song. Chorus D will choose a happy song. After the choruses have practiced for a few minutes, read aloud the following story, signaling choruses to sing as noted. **Once upon a time, there was a guy named Bob. Bob was a brilliant child. You could tell, because every day he sang this song.** (Chorus A sings.) **As he grew, Bob became strong and almost handsome. He met Roberta, a beautiful young woman. Asking her to marry him, he sang . . .** (Chorus B sings.) **But she said no. Bob was so miserable that all he could do was stand in the middle of the mall, singing . . .** (Chorus C sings.) **After he sang, Bob was taken away by a mall security guard named Babs. She asked Bob to marry her, and they were so happy that they sang . . .** (Chorus D sings.) **Bob and Babs lived happily ever after.** Give prizes for best singing and most appropriate song. Then discuss the part music plays in the high and low points of our lives.

Step 3

To make Steps 3 and 4 more involving, offer a piece of candy or gum to anyone who answers a discussion question. But offer *two* pieces to anyone who answers a question with a song title or a phrase from a song (which must be sung). For example, for **Describe the influence Solomon's wives had on him**, an answer might be "Love Potion #9" or "Under My Thumb." For **Who or what has an influence on you?** an answer might be, "Your Mama Don't Dance and Your Daddy Don't Rock and Roll." Accept one song reference per question.

Step 3

If kids have grown defensive at hearing their music criticized in church, the story of Solomon probably won't help. Instead, accentuate the positive with a reading of Psalm 98. Discuss its encouragement to praise God through music in new ways. Let kids list ways in which their favorite musical styles could be used in church. Ask: **Should church music be more like the music you listen to the rest of the week? If so, is the reverse true? Should we apply what we claim to believe in church to the music we listen to the rest of the week? If not, are we being hypocritical?** Use this discussion as a bridge to Step 4.

Step 4

Kids may have heard these "music influences you" and discussions before. Try something else instead. Start with your version of the Grammy Awards—the Granny Awards. Explain that these awards are given to recording artists that grandmothers would like teenagers to listen to. Ask kids to nominate and vote on two in each of these categories: Male Artist, Female Artist, and Group. Then ask: **How do adults think your music influences you? Can you be a hundred percent sure that song lyrics and music influence nobody?** Read Philippians 1:9-11. Ask: **What does discern mean?** (Sort out; tell the difference; judge.) **On what bases— keyboard skills, originality, etc.—do you discern what music is best? How could you include qualities like purity and blamelessness in your judgments?** Read I Corinthians 2:11-16. Ask: **Since only you know what thoughts music brings to your mind, how will you deal with music that encourages the wrong kinds of thoughts? How interested are you in what God's Spirit thinks of your musical choices? Do you have "the mind of Christ" when it comes to music? Explain.**

Step 3

Prefer to study passages that require less explanation? Use the "Combined Junior High/High School" option for Step 3. You may also want to give this quick true-false quiz about music in the Bible. **(1) The Book of Psalms is a collection of songs written by David.** (Partly false. Asaph and possibly others contributed some too.) **(2) The Song of Songs, also known as Song of Solomon, is a love song written by, for, or about King Solomon.** (True.) **(3) There are no songs in the New Testament.** (False. There are a lot of them. Several characters—like Mary and Zechariah in Luke 1, and probably angels and Simeon in Luke 2—were so full of praise for God that they broke into song.) **(4) The Book of Revelation includes songs that will be sung in heaven** (True. See Revelation 5 and 15.) **(5) The Bible instructs us to sing only to God.** (False. See Ephesians 5:19.)

Step 4

To many kids, the Philippians 4:8, 9 qualities seem to run together in a hard-to-distinguish, hard-to-apply mass of "niceness." Here are some meanings of the original Greek terms, which you may want to share. *True*—not concealing. *Noble*—honest. *Right*—fair, innocent, just. *Pure*—clean, modest. *Lovely*—friendly toward, acceptable. *Admirable*—well spoken of, having a good reputation. *Excellent*—virtue, praise. *Praiseworthy*—commendable.

Step 1

Try the following getting-to-know-you opener. Have each person bring a favorite song on tape. Collect the tapes and mix them up. Play about 30 seconds of each song; then have kids guess whose song is whose. Give each person a chance to explain briefly why the song or style is special to him or her.

Step 5

Begin your worship time with this scenario: **Let's say you're in love. You write to your boyfriend or girlfriend, who's going to school in Europe for a semester. Instead of sending the letter, you get a friend with a nice voice to read it on tape. Then, instead of sending the tape, you just keep it and listen to it over and over. Would there be anything strange about that? Why?** Explain that this is how some of us "worship" with music—instead of sending our musical messages to God, we just listen to others singing on albums, on the platform, or in the next pew. Encourage kids to worship God directly with music. Give them a chance to do so by singing songs directed to God ("I Love You, Lord," "It Is You," "Great Is Thy Faithfulness," etc.).

Step 3

After discussing the influences that changed Solomon's relationship with God, talk about the ability we have to be an influence. Have group member form two teams. Then present this discussion statement: **It is not possible to influence a friend without his or her being aware of your influence.** Assign one team to speak in agreement with the statement and the other to speak against it. Ask the teams to list a few examples to support their position and then choose three or four members to serve on a debate panel to discuss the positions and examples for the entire group.

Step 4

Have group members form eight teams. Give each team one of the words from Philippians 4:8. Ask the teams to define their word and then think of some specific examples of songs that illustrate the word. (The illustrations could be both positive and negative.) For example, you might ask: **What music is appropriate to listen to when you want to think praise-worthy thoughts? What music is *not* appropriate for thinking praisewor-thy thoughts?** Ask the teams to share their definitions and examples with each other.

Step 3

Make the most of guys' ability to identify with Solomon's problem. Make three signs that say, "Yeah, Sure," "For the Right Person, Maybe," and "No Way!" Post these on the wall. To start Step 3, say: **Let's say you have a really great-looking girlfriend. Here's a list of things you might be willing to do to please her. After each item, stand under the sign that shows your reaction. (1) Eat Chinese food—all vegetables. (2) Sit through an opera once a month. (3) Walk a mile in a snowstorm to buy a pair of shoes she wants. (4) Promise never to grow a beard. (5) Change diapers in the church nursery every week. (6) Throw away all your tapes and CDs. (7) Get her name tattooed on your chest. (8) Become a Buddhist.** Then ask: **How did you decide to draw the line between "Maybe" and "No Way"? Why are most guys willing to please their girlfriends by doing things they wouldn't normally do?** Then read about Solomon's situation. Ask: **How might certain kinds of music, like Solomon's wives, influence a guy to do things he normally wouldn't do?**

Step 4

Guys may think Philippians 4:8, 9 sounds "feminine," even though it's addressed to "brothers." Help them associate these traits with "guy stuff" by having a scavenger hunt. Give two teams several magazines read mostly by males (*Sports Illustrated, Field and Stream, Motor Trend, Business Week,* etc.). The first team to find an event or object representing each of the eight Philippians qualities wins. For example, "pure" could be represented by a photo of a mountain stream or an article about highly refined gasoline. "Noble" might be represented by a story about a wilderness rescue or an athlete's work for charity. Allow five to ten minutes for the hunt; then have the teams share their results.

Step 1

Bring an electronic keyboard, the widely used kind that provides accompaniment in a variety of rhythms (rock, country, march, disco, waltz, etc.). Make sure that you, a group member, or a guest can play a familiar tune. Have group members form teams. Each team will sing along with the keyboard for one minute. During that time, change the rhythm and tempo of the accompaniment frequently and without warning. The team that does the best job of keeping up is the winner. After the contest, ask: **Which of these rhythms seemed to work best with this song? Which rhythm do you usually like best? Why?**

Step 5

Have group members form teams. Give each team a sheet of paper and a pen. At your signal, teams will come up with names of musical groups that fit these categories: (1) groups with animal names (Los Lobos, Turtles, Eagles, Scorpions, Animals, Monkees, etc.); (2) groups with "boys" or "girls" in their names (Indigo Girls, Beach Boys, Boyz 2 Men, Oak Ridge Boys, Beastie Boys, etc.); (3) names referring to inanimate objects (Guns 'n' Roses, Rolling Stones, Red Hot Chili Peppers, The Doors, etc.); (4) names including at least three initials or numbers (INXS, R.E.M., XTC, REO Speedwagon, B-52s, AC/DC, etc.). The first team to get four names in all categories wins. Then ask: **What groups would you put in this category: the best groups for Christians to listen to? Why?**

Step 2

During the week, record five or ten seconds each from ten TV series theme songs. Choose shows that most kids will be familiar with. At this point in the meeting, pass out paper. Have kids number their papers from 1 to 10. As you play your tape, kids should write down their guesses as to which shows the songs come from. Give a prize to the person who gets the most right. Then discuss: **What feeling do you get when you hear a song from a show that you like? What mental image do you get?** Move into a discussion of favorite music styles and the power of music.

Step 4

Before the session, tape or rent some music videos—the kind shown on MTV. At this point in the meeting, play portions of several—but with the sound off. As you do, ask kids which artists' clothes have influenced or might influence fashion. After viewing the videos, note that some kids who are really into certain kinds of music wear clothes that their favorite performers wear. Ask group members to list some currently hot looks that musicians have helped to make popular. Then ask: **What does this say about the way music and musicians can influence us? Do you think this influence is healthy or not?**

Step 1

Combine Steps 1 and 2 in a brief opener. Bring a big sack of records, tapes, or CDs—from your collection or borrowed from others. Have two kids play Santa Claus and pass out albums to the kids they think would like them most (or hate them least). Ask your Santas: **How did you decide who should get each album?** Ask recipients: **What album would you have preferred? What album are you glad you didn't get? Why? How would you describe your favorite style of music in one word?** Be sure to collect the albums before moving to the next step (unless you're trying to get rid of them).

Step 4

Skip the ranking of influences and the questions that appear before the reading of the Philippians passage. Have group members form three teams—one representing hard rock, one representing country music, and one representing Top 40. Each team will come up with (1) one way in which its style could be to a Christian as Solomon's wives were to him; (2) one song or group that seems to be an exception to that generalization; and (3) a decision as to whether Jesus would listen to that style, and if so, how many hours a week He might spend on it. After a few minutes, have the teams share their results. Then read and discuss Philippians 4:8, 9.

Step 2

Give each group member a large sheet of paper and a pencil. You will play several styles of music—including rap, rhythm and blues, reggae, country, hard rock, heavy metal, jazz, gospel, and classical. After you play each style, group members will judge the style according to how well they like it. To indicate their responses, group members will write a number between one and ten on their sheets. "One" means they hate that style; "ten" means they love it. Ask volunteers to explain their responses.

Step 4

Some city teens face a dilemma when it comes to practicing Christianity and listening to certain music. Some choose to avoid secular music completely and listen only to Christian music. However, many live in environments where they cannot just turn off certain secular songs. They may live in a community in which music is literally blaring in the streets, or in households in which the music selection this is beyond their control. Comfort these teens with understanding that Jesus recognizes that sometimes we must practice moral excellence while living in a musical swamp. Review one possible response to this type of situation in Matthew 15:11, 17-20a.

COMBINED

Step 1
Try a simpler, more active opener. As kids enter, give each an index card with a description of a person (history teacher, auto mechanic, pastor, two year old, senior citizen, student body president, drug dealer, etc.) on it. Have four tape players going, each in a corner. One should play rock; one classical music; one hymns; one rap or rhythm and blues. Each person should move to the corner that he or she thinks the person on the card would be attracted to. Once kids are in their corners, see whether their characters have much in common. Ask: **Why did you go to the corner you went to? Do you like the music that adults think "all kids" like? What happens when we think we know more about other people's styles than we really do?** (We judge them, stereotype them, etc.)

Step 3
Younger kids may miss the connection between Solomon and music. You may want to try a more straightforward study. Ask: **Why do you like the music you like?** (It makes me feel good.) **How do you think God feels about that?** Read the following passages, which connect music with good feelings and enthusiasm. I Chronicles 13:8. Ask: **Does this sound like the way our group uses music? What kinds of music help you celebrate?** Psalm 45:8. Ask: **What music makes you glad? Could you thank God for it, even if it isn't church music? How?** Psalm 108:1. Ask: **When have you made music with all of your soul? How did it feel?** Psalm 135:3. Ask: **Is singing praises pleasant to you? Why or why not?** James 5:13. Ask: **Does happiness lead you to singing, or the other way around? What songs could you sing when you're happy?** Revelation 5:11, 12. Ask: **How would you fit into this scene? Why?**

EXTRA CHALLENGE

Step 1
The following opener may provoke more thought on the part of your group members. Have them form four teams. Explain that each team is starting a radio station. Team A is a country station; Team B is "classic rock"; Team C is cutting-edge rock; Team D wants to play only songs that have the word *honey* in them. Teams must answer these questions: **What call letters would you like your station to have?** (For stations east of the Mississippi, the first of the four call letters must be W. For stations west of the Mississippi, the first letter must be K.) **How might a typical disc jockey on your station sound? What might be a typical disc jockey name on your station? Who do you think would want to advertise on your station in the following categories, and why: clothing stores, restaurants, movies, TV shows, cosmetics?** After a few minutes, have the teams share their responses. Then discuss the assumptions people make about fans of various kinds of music. Note that radio stations and music companies spend big bucks to find out all about people who like different styles.

Step 5
See how many kids are willing to let you or one of the other group leaders look at their music collections at home and evaluate them. Discuss the pros and cons of doing that. If anyone is willing to let you or someone else look at his or her music, arrange to do it this week. Here are some questions to ask during such an evaluation: **Which three albums do you listen to most? Why? Are there any songs on those albums that you wouldn't want me to hear? Are there any album covers you wouldn't want other family members to see? Would you play one of your favorite songs for me? Can you find at least one song on each album that fits Philippians 4:8, 9?**

PLANNING CHECKLIST

Date Used:

Approx. Time

Step 1: Let's Do Lunch _____
o Extra Action
o Small Group
o Large Group
o Fellowship & Worship
o Extra Fun
o Short Meeting Time
o Combined Junior High/High School
o Extra Challenge
Things needed:

Step 2: What's with Music? _____
o Extra Action
o Media
o Urban
Things needed:

Step 3: Under the Influence _____
o Large Group
o Heard It All Before
o Little Bible Background
o Mostly Girls
o Mostly Guys
o Combined Junior High/High School
Things needed:

Step 4: An Influential Tune _____
o Heard It All Before
o Little Bible Background
o Mostly Girls
o Mostly Guys
o Media
o Short Meeting Time
o Urban
Things needed:

Step 5: Check That Dial _____
o Small Group
o Fellowship & Worship
o Extra Fun
o Extra Challenge
Things needed:

A Look of Your Own

☐ To help kids see how easy it is to convince themselves that image is everything—even when it's not.

☐ To help kids understand that God created them with great worth and value.

☐ To help kids determine whether or not they have to look a certain way.

☐ Other _____
_____

Your Bible Base:

1 Samuel 16:1-13
Psalm 139:1-4, 13-16

Image Is Everything

(Needed: Copies of Repro Resource 4)

Distribute copies of "Image, Center Court" (Repro Resource 4). Assign four group members to play the leading roles in the skit. Everyone else in the group will be the crowd.

Give group members a chance to read through the skit once; then have them perform. Encourage them to have fun with their parts, whether they're acting out the tennis match or being super-enthusiastic spectators.

When the skit is over, discuss it, using the following questions.

Why wasn't this an even tennis match? (Jimmy didn't have a chance, because all that mattered was image, which Andy had.)

Who seemed to be the better tennis player? Did this fact make a difference? Why or why not? (Jimmy seemed to be the better player, but the game wasn't based on skill or talent, just image.)

In the skit, Andy made a comment about knowing a great image consultant. Suppose Jimmy wanted to get a total image make-over so he could look and be exactly like Andy. What would the pros and cons of doing this? Let group members weigh the issue of imitating someone else's style.

Then say: **In the real world, image often is everything, but is it really *everything*?**

First Impressions

(Needed: Photographs of people you know, but your group members don't)

Say: **When you see someone for the first time, do you usually form an opinion about him or her, without even talking to the person? Can you think of a time when you did**

this, and the person turned out to be completely different from your first impression? Encourage several group members to talk about their experiences.

Then take out some photos of people you know. Don't let on that these people are friends or family members. As the group members pass the photos around, have them guess things about the people, based on appearance alone.

After everyone has seen the photos, collect them, and tell your group members who the people in the photos are and what they're really like.

If some of your group members' impressions were fairly accurate, point that out. Then explain: **When I look at these pictures, I see my friends and family members. I know who they are, what they like and don't like. I might notice appearances, like my dad looks older now than he did when the picture was taken, but that's not my only impression of him.**

Why is there so much emphasis on appearance and image in our society? Let group members voice their opinions. If no one mentions it, suggest that the world is a more visual place than ever before. Television, movies, and magazines powerfully communicate messages of success and beauty that usually are based on some unattainable standard of perfection.

It's kind of funny the way advertisers try to package and sell a "unique" look to millions of people. Hello? What do you think? Does this strategy work? Does it make sense? Encourage group members to talk about some of the looks they like as well as the pressures they feel to buy into a current look.

Is it wrong to buy into this package? Is it ever right? Why or why not? (It might be wrong if you honestly don't like something, but felt pressured to wear it—or if the look were totally wrong for you. On the other hand, it's fine to wear things that are in style, as long as you don't get obsessed with them.)

If someone wanders into a bookstore without knowing exactly what he or she wants, he or she might tend to judge a book by its cover. But a cool-looking cover doesn't guarantee a good story. In the same way, our outside packaging— our appearance—needs to reflect who we are.

Friend and Creator

(Needed: Bibles)

OPTIONS

EXTRA ACTION

HEARD IT ALL BEFORE

LITTLE BIBLE BACKGROUND

MOSTLY GIRLS

EXTRA CHALLENGE

Point out that God sees us from the inside out. Have group members turn to I Samuel 16:1-13. Ask volunteers to take turns reading this story of how the Lord instructed Samuel to choose David to succeed Saul as king of Israel.

Explain: **Eliab obviously made an impression on Samuel. He probably was good-looking, tall, and seemed perfect. Do you think Samuel may have wondered why the Lord passed over someone so obviously qualified to be king?** (Samuel probably had preconceived notions of what a king should look like, especially since Saul had been good-looking and tall too.)

The key to the passage is verse 7. What does this verse tell us? (The Lord has a different perspective than we do. We might be impressed by a person's looks and appearance, but the Lord is more concerned about a person's heart and what his or her character is like.)

How does this verse apply when you feel the pressure to look good or you feel rotten because you don't look good? What difference does it make to know that the Lord isn't evaluating you on the basis of your looks? Actually the real question has to do with a person's self-worth and value in Christ, which thankfully have nothing to do with weight, height, or physical appearance.

Say: **The Lord knows us, because He created us.** Have volunteers read aloud Psalm 139:1-4, 13-16.

Describe the imagery David used to describe how God made each of us. (David describes God as knitting and weaving us together in our mothers' wombs. It sounds like the work of an artist or designer.)

Even when we're not sure about ourselves and how we look, God is sure. We're more than a random mixture of genes; we were carefully designed by God. We are fearfully and wonderfully made by Him.

How does this make you feel about yourself? How does it make you feel about God? Encourage group members to talk about their feelings. Psalm 139 can be a wonderful tonic for the "Don't-like-myself blues."

Obsession

(Needed: Pencils, copies of Repro Resource 5)

Have group members form three teams. Distribute pencils and copies of "Casting Call" (Repro Resource 5) to each team. Read aloud the instructions for the sheet. Then give the teams a few minutes to work on it.

When everyone is finished, have the teams read aloud their character descriptions. Note similarities or differences in the descriptions.

Then say: **Suppose Cindy and Dylan start to get obsessed with their looks. Let's take your descriptions of Cindy and Dylan to their extremes.**

Explain that you want the teams to try to top each other's obsessions. For example, let's say one team decides that Cindy wakes up one day and decides her nose is too big for her face, so she schedules cosmetic surgery. The next team might say that, afterward, Cindy's mouth and eyes no longer fit with her new nose, so she has plastic surgery done on those. The third team might say that Cindy keeps on having reconstructive surgery until she winds up looking like Michael Jackson.

Encourage the teams to think of wild and crazy obsessions—anything to make these two characters look absurd.

Then ask: **What's happened to these beautiful people? Could they have survived just the way they were? Why or why not?** Point out that when we become obsessed with our image and looks, we might throw all common sense out the window, and end up worse off than we were before.

Your Own Good Looks

Say: **Think about yourself. How do you think you look? How do you think the other people here think you look? How do**

OPTIONS

you think God thinks you look? Let group members answer aloud if they want to, but don't force anyone to respond.

What are some things you do to make yourself look good? Encourage group members to focus on things that don't cost a lot of money or require hours and hours of preparation—things like practicing personal hygiene, wearing clean clothes, maintaining proper posture, smiling frequently, etc. The point is that anyone can look good without spending a small fortune.

Then say: **Look at the other people here. Each of us has been created individually and specially by God. Think of unusual, but positive, compliments you can pay each other. What is it that you like about each other?** Explain that the compliments can be about anything but physical characteristics. Encourage group members to exchange their compliments with each other. It's important that you make sure everyone in the group receives compliments. Don't worry if some of the compliments are off the wall—as long as they're not thinly disguised insults.

Close the session in prayer, thanking God for creating all of you with great worth and value. Ask the Lord to help your group members develop the right perspective on their appearance.

Image, Center Court

ANNOUNCER: Good afternoon, everybody, and welcome to Wimblyton. Today you'll see top-seeded Andy Argoosey take on first-time tennis sensation Jimmy Rockers in the match of the decade. Andy, can we get a few words with you?

ANDY *(all smiles)*: Image is everything. *(The crowd goes wild.)*

ANNOUNCER: Thank you, Andy. And Jimmy, can we have a few words with you?

JIMMY: Sure. It's an honor to be playing here in one of the great sports arenas of all time. It reminds me of the time when my Uncle Stuffy…

ANNOUNCER: Sorry, Jimmy, but we're out of time for you; the match is about to begin.

LINE JUDGE: Players to center court!

(Andy and Jimmy stand next to each other.)

LINE JUDGE: Remember that my job is to be fair. So let's have a good match because…

ANDY: Image is everything! *(The crowd goes wild again.)*

ANNOUNCER: The players take their positions. Andy serves first. What a powerful swing! The ball sails over Jimmy's head.

LINE JUDGE: In! Point to Argoosey!

JIMMY: What!? That ball was ten feet over my head!

LINE JUDGE: Yes, that's true, but…

ANDY: Image is everything! *(The crowd goes berserk.)*

LINE JUDGE: Serve to Rockers.

ANNOUNCER: Jimmy has got incredible talent. He makes the ball spin like a top. Here's his serve. Just inside the line!

LINE JUDGE: Out! Point to Argoosey!

JIMMY: What!!? That serve was perfect!

LINE JUDGE: Yes, that's true, but…

ANDY: Image is everything! *(The crowd goes nuts.)*

LINE JUDGE: Game goes to Argoosey!

(Raises Andy's arm into the air.)

JIMMY: This is ridiculous! I got all the points! I've got all the skill, the talent, the originality! And you just look good!

ANDY: Sorry, pal, but like I said…

ANNOUNCER, LINE JUDGE, ANDY, CROWD: Image is everything!

ANDY: Hey, Jimmy, I know a great image consultant.

ANNOUNCER: And there it is! Victory again for Andy Argoosey, once more proving that image is everything.

Casting Call

The storyline for a new TV sitcom involves Cindy and Dylan, who are neighbors in an apartment complex. He works in a men's clothing store. She works in a weight-loss center. They're both aerobics instructors. The show centers on their good looks and cheerful outlooks on life.

Below are call sheets for the actor and actress who will eventually play the parts. Give as many details as possible to help them know how to play their characters. If you'd like, sketch out how you think Cindy and Dylan should look.

Describe their looks, the specific brands of clothes they wear, how they wear their hair, what shampoo they use, what makeup she uses, where they shop, and anything else you can think of.

Dylan Brock   **Cindy Sherman**

Step 1

Bring four empty, medium-sized cardboard cartons. Each should be taped shut, with a foot-sized hole cut in the top. Say: **You've heard of the Pump. This is the Box. Cool people wear Boxes. To be cool, wear them during this relay race.** Racers on two teams will take turns wearing the boxes over their shoes, shuffling to the opposite wall and back. Afterward, discuss how far some kids go to look cool. In Step 2, have group members form two teams. Give each team a paper plate and a glue stick. The teams will hunt for eyes, nose, and mouth (which you've cut from magazine photos and hidden around your meeting place beforehand). The first team to glue the right number of features on its "face" (the plate) and bring it to you wins. Afterward, discuss how kids search for the right look, trying out different clothes, hairstyles, etc. Ask: **What "looks" have you tried? Have you found the "right" look? Do you think you ever will?**

Step 3

Have kids act out the I Samuel passage as it's read. In Step 4, draw two faces on a chalkboard. Have group members form two teams. Assign each team a face. The first person on each team will take a piece of chalk, run to the board, change one feature of the face, and bring the chalk back to the next person, who will do the same thing. The team with the "best looking" face in two minutes wins. Afterward, discuss extreme efforts (cosmetic surgery, etc.) to change one's appearance. In Step 5, give two teams an equal number of coins—including foreign coins and one worth more than face value (such as an Indian head penny). Teams will have one minute to arrange their coins "in order of value"—which will be tough to do unless kids know how much each coin is worth. Use this to illustrate the fact that every person exceeds "face value."

Step 1

If the skit requires more actors than you can muster, try an "ugly face contest" instead. Bring old magazines, paper plates, scissors, and glue sticks. Have kids cut parts of faces from the magazines and glue them together on the plates to make the worst-looking faces they can. Kids can mix parts of features too—big nostrils on a small nose, for instance. After five minutes, display the results. Choose (or let kids choose) the ugliest face; award a prize to its maker. Then ask: **What's your definition of *ugly*? Of *beautiful*? Have you ever felt like parts of your face or your body don't quite go to-gether? What made you feel that way? Do you think other kids feel that way? Why or why not?**

Step 5

Members of a small group may feel awkward (and coerced) if they suddenly have to compliment each other. Try a variation of the old "shell game" instead. Bring three opaque cups. Before the session, put the cups on a tray with a small object (peanut, ball, etc.) under each cup. Cover the cups with a cloth. Keep the whole thing out of sight. At this point in the meeting, remove the cloth and say: **Heard of the old shell game? A con artist has three containers, puts an object under one of them, and moves them around like this** (slide the cups around, changing their order repeatedly). **You're supposed to bet on where the object is—but the con artist has a hole in the table, and the object is never under the container you choose.** Ask three volunteers to guess which cup has an object under it. Then reveal that *all* the cups do. Use this to illustrate the fact that *every* person is special inside, no matter how things look on the outside.

Step 2

Unless you have a lot of pictures, passing them around may take longer than the discussion. Instead, post ten photos (your own or ones of nonfamous people you've cut from magazines and newspapers) of adults on numbered sheets of paper around the room. Make sure you know the occupation of each person in the photos, and that the photos don't reveal the occupations. Write the occupations under the wrong photos. For example, if you have photos of a basketball coach, a dog trainer, and a ballet dancer, you might write "Dog Trainer" under the coach, "Ballet Dancer" under the dog trainer, and "Basketball Coach" under the ballet dancer. Have kids walk around with sheets of paper numbered from I to 10 and write down their guesses as to which people go with which occupations. Whoever gets the most right answers wins. Then discuss the tendency to judge by appearance.

Step 5

Can you guarantee that everyone in your group will get a compliment? If not, try the following activity. Stage a "fashion show" that has nothing to do with clothes. Kids will line up and walk one at a time, as if they were fashion models, down a "runway" (an area at the front of the room). You will act as announcer. As each person comes down the runway, you will describe an inner quality or ability that each person is "wearing." The rest of the group will then applaud. (For example: **Jeremy is wearing the willingness to help out on short notice, as we all saw at the picnic when the hamburgers fell in the river. Vanessa sports a stunning ability to make visitors feel right at home.**) Outline in advance what you'll say about each person. For added atmosphere, play upbeat music in the background and take flash pictures of your "models."

Step 3

Since I Samuel 16:7 and Psalm 139 have often been applied to self-image, kids may consider them old news. Instead, look at how Jesus addressed the issue of "image." Read Matthew 6:16-18. Ask: **What image were the hypocrites trying to project? What do kids today try to project through their looks?** Read Matthew 11:7-11. Ask: **Based on this passage, what do you think Jesus would say about slogans like "Dress for success" and "Clothes make the man"? What does verse 11 say about the value of every believer?** Read Matthew 23:5-12. Ask: **Why did these religious leaders like to wear fancy clothes? Is that why kids today wear them? Based on verses 5 and 12, what might Jesus think of bodybuilding contests, beauty pageants, and your clothes closet?** Read Matthew 23:27, 28. Ask: **How does the amount of time spent on your "outside" each week compare with that spent on the "inside"?** Read John 19:23, 24. Ask: **How do you feel about the importance of clothes after reading these verses? Why?**

Step 5

Kids may be thinking, "So what if God created me? I still have to look good." Ask: **What happens to people who don't have the "right" look?** Discuss the fact that most of us want to look "right" so that we'll get things we feel we need—friends, love, respect, good times, boyfriend or girlfriend, the right job, etc. We trust our looks to get us those things—more than we trust God to give us what we need no matter how we look. Read Matthew 6:25-34. Ask kids to talk honestly with God about their concerns over what they might not get because of the way they look. Offer to talk later with anyone who needs help with this.

Step 3

Kids may get a mixed message from the I Samuel passage. God's choice may not have been the handsome Eliab, but David was handsome too (vs. 12). That could leave kids—especially those who don't have broader knowledge of the Bible— thinking that God really does favor good-looking people. As needed, draw kids' attention to others in the Bible who were valued despite their appearance: Zacchaeus, who was short (Luke 19:1-10); Mephibosheth, who was disabled (II Samuel 9); Jesus, who was foreseen as having no beauty or desirability (Isaiah 53:2); and those without nice clothes (James 2:1-5).

Step 5

The question of how God thinks we look is a tough one for anybody—especially for kids without much Bible knowledge. Here are some ideas you may want to share. God was pleased with the first people He made (Genesis 1:27-31). He's much more interested in what's going on in a person's mind and heart than with what he or she looks like (Matthew 23:27, 28). He sees things from an eternal perspective, so He knows how we'll look when we're more mature (Psalm 139:16) and He knows that these bodies are only temporary (Luke 20:34-38). He knows every detail of our appearance (Matthew 10:30). No matter how we look, He loves us (I John 3:1) and wants to be close to us (James 4:8).

Step 1

Try the following relational opener. Have group members form pairs. Instruct partners to guess five things that are now in each other's pockets, purses, or wallets. Then have each partner show whether the guesser was right or wrong. Ask: **Why did you guess as you did?** (Girls/guys always carry that stuff around; he/she looked like the kind of person who would have that; etc.) Use this as an example of judging what's inside when all you really know is the "outward appearance."

Step 5

Have kids put on choir robes (borrowed from your church or another church). Ask: **Why do choirs wear robes?** (To lessen the distraction of "street clothes"; to make choir members look alike; to emphasize the special nature of worship; etc.) **What if everybody in church wore robes like these? Would that make it easier for you to worship by getting rid of the distraction of regular clothes? Or would worship be harder because you'd feel self-conscious? Does dressing up for church distract you from the real reason you're there, or does it put you in the right "mood" for worship?** Try singing a chorus with and without the robes. Discuss how it felt. Then, in regular clothes, sing some of your favorite praise songs—encouraging kids to forget the way they look and concentrate on God.

Step 3

As you talk about Eliab and Samuel, point out the hidden impressions we live with as a part of modern culture. Say: **Valid studies show that individuals who are physically taller and more "attractive" than the average person advance more rapidly in business and gain unearned advantages not appropriate for their education or skill level. How does this affect your attitude toward yourself? Toward others?** Discuss the differences between this image of a person's value and God's standard of a person's value.

Step 4

As you distribute copies of "Casting Call" (Repro Resource 5), explain to your group members that the character of Dylan Brock has been changed to be an attorney named Dyla Brock. Dyla is an aggressive professional who will use her good looks and fashion awareness to create a successful presence in the courtroom.

Step 2

Talk specifically about what makes up the right "guy image" at the moment. Bring a disposable razor, a bottle of cologne, acne medicine, hairstyling gel or spray, suntan lotion, and ads for the following: workout equipment or bodybuilding supplies; guys' shirts, pants, jackets, shoes, and jewelry. Give one item to each group member. Each person must answer the following questions about his item: **Is using this item "in" or "out" right now? If it's "in," how and when is it to be used and/or worn? On a scale of 1 to 10—with 10 being highest—how necessary is this item to the right "guy image"? If the item is "out," what has replaced it? Why?** Encourage other group members to explain whether they agree or disagree with each person's responses.

Step 5

Guys' competitiveness or unwillingness to show emotion may keep them from wanting to compliment each other. Try an alternative. Address guys' struggles over the awkwardness, skin problems, and beardless faces they may have now. During the week before the session, collect as many high school photos of men in your church as you can. Show them to guys now and note that at least *some* of them improved with age. Ask: **What's one thing you hope you grow out of or into? If that doesn't change, would you be willing to trust God to help you survive anyway?**

Step 1

Start with a "bad haircut contest." Bring two cheap wigs (perhaps from secondhand stores or garage sales), two tablecloths, and two pairs of blunt scissors. Get four volunteers—two to be "stylists" and two to be "victims." Be sure the victims' hair is shorter than that of the wigs. Seat the victims at the front of the room. Put the wigs on their heads and cover their clothes with the tablecloths, barber-style. Give each stylist a pair of scissors. At your signal, stylists will compete to create the worst-looking haircut (cutting only the wigs, of course) in ninety seconds. Let the rest of the group vote to choose the winner. After awarding prizes to the winning stylist and victim, ask: **How do you feel when you get a bad haircut? What happens when you have a "bad hair day"? Have you ever thought you looked awful, but someone else said you looked fine? What do you think caused the difference of opinion?**

Step 5

Give each group member an apple. Instruct each person to "sculpt" a self-portrait from the apple, using only his or her teeth. After two or three minutes, call a halt to the sculpting. Have kids display their handiwork on a table. Let everyone view the results; see whether kids can match apples with sculptors. Award a prize for the most detailed sculpture. Point out that just as the apples don't quite resemble their sculptors, our self-images often don't match our real images. The One who "sculpted" us—God—is the best judge of what we're really worth.

Step 1

Rent movies on video that depict the way some young people looked during past decades. (Examples: *Boys' Town* [1930s]; any Andy Hardy movie [1940s]; *Rebel without a Cause* [1950s]; *Hair* [1960s]; *Saturday Night Fever* [1970s]; *Footloose* [1980s]. (Note: Be sure to preview the scenes you plan to show.) Play an appropriate scene from each film. Discuss how people looked (clothes, hairstyles, makeup, etc.). Ask: **Which "looks" seemed OK to you? Which did you dislike most? When you realize that today's hot looks will be outdated tomorrow, how does it make you feel? If you could pick any look you wanted, regardless of time, what would it be? What keeps you from looking that way?**

Step 4

Play a couple of songs that talk about physical appearance. If you can't find current examples, here are some oldies you might use: "Material Girl" (Madonna), "At Seventeen" (Janis Ian), "Legs" (ZZ Top); "Oh, Pretty Woman" (Roy Orbison). Then ask: **What attitude does the songwriter seem to have about physical beauty? How does it compare with what the Bible says? How do most popular songs treat the subject of looks? Are most of them about girls or guys? Why do you think that is?**

Step 1

Combine Steps 1 and 2 in this opener. Pass around a rose. Have kids try to top each other in saying how ugly it is. ("You're so ugly you make artificial flowers look good"; "Is that a petal—or are you eating a rotten strawberry?") Say: **No matter what we say, the rose is beautiful. But what if somebody decides all flowers should look like daisies? Does the rose become defective?** (No.) Note that our value doesn't change either—no matter what people say about our looks, no matter how standards of beauty change. Ask: **What's the "right" way for guys to look right now? What about girls? Who decided this? On a scale of 1 to 10—with 10 being the highest—how much pressure do you feel to look that way? On the same scale, how hard would it be for you to look that way?**

Step 4

Combine Steps 4 and 5 in the following way. Say: **Each of you has $3,000. You can buy only one of these things: an all-new wardrobe, plastic surgery on your face, a ten-year membership at a health club, or a perfect complexion. Which do you choose? Why?** If kids don't want to answer for themselves, let them say which they think is most valuable and why. Then ask: **How much does each of these cost: good posture, a smile, baths or showers, exercising on your own, going on a diet, looking others in the eye and showing an interest in them, combing or brushing your hair, brushing your teeth?** Have each person complete this sentence for a partner: **One free thing I can do this week to feel more confident about the way I look is . . .** Point out one more free thing kids can do by reading 1 Peter 3:3, 4. Encourage them to see growing in Christ as a way to look better outwardly as well as inwardly.

Step 2

Another way to deal with first impressions is to see how kids judge books by their covers. Display ten books, which kids will help you put in order of perceived importance. But there's one catch: Kids can't get out of their seats and you can't open the books. They will make their decisions based the covers. Choose an array of books: new and old, thick and thin, paperback and clothbound, ones with pictures on the covers and ones with no pictures, ones with grandiose titles and ones with simple titles. One of the books should be a Bible that is disguised and tattered with no name on the binder. Let your group members help you categorize the books by a majority vote. The object is to see where they place the Bible in the set. Afterward, discuss the implications of simply judging a book by its cover.

Step 5

If your group members know each other well and want to do a positive affirmation activity, try this. Before the group arrives, prepare on separate sheets of paper the names of each member. When you begin, hand out to each person a name that he or she will keep secret. Then have group members write (1) three examples of inner beauty about their person, and (2) three ways they think their person would use his or her inner beauty to improve the city if he or she were the mayor. Collect the papers (with no names on them) and read the compliments back to the group. Before closing with prayer, see if anyone wants to reveal whose name they had in an attempt to build greater fellowship.

Step 1
Replace the skit with a more concrete activity. Bring a movie magazine, eyebrow pencil, lipstick, makeup remover, and a large bag of small candies. See how much candy it takes to bribe volunteers to look "dumb." Issue these challenges, letting one person take you up on each: **(1) Show the group your bare feet. (2) Wear your socks as "puppets" on your hands and make them sing "Three Blind Mice." (3) Get down on all fours and "oink" like a pig for ten seconds. (4) Let another group member mess up your hair. (5) Kiss a magazine picture of a movie star. (6) Let another group member make you up to look like a clown.** Then ask which stunt looked "dumbest." Talk about how we hate to look dumb or out of place. Ask kids to name a time when something about their appearance made them feel like they didn't fit in.

Step 5
Try a hands-on closing. Bring two or three inflated mylar balloons, the kind with silvery, reflective plastic on one side (available in party shops and toy stores). Have kids pass the balloons around as you play recorded music. When you stop the music, kids holding the balloons must look closely at their faces in the "mirror" side and describe how they look. (Noses and other features will be exaggerated in the curved "mirror.") Ask: **If this were the only mirror you ever had, how might you feel about your appearance?** Then play the music again and give a couple of other kids a chance to look and reply. Point out that just as the balloon enlarged parts of kids' reflections, we tend to blow our "defects" out of proportion. When we see ourselves as God sees us, we get a true picture.

Step 3
Add a study on clothes. Have teams split up the following passages and answer the accompanying questions. *Genesis 37:3, 4.* **What feelings can clothes create in those who make or give them? In those who get them—or don't get them?** *Exodus 35:20-23.* **What did the Israelites do with some of their clothes? Why? Based on this passage, would you say God is for or against nice clothes? Why?** *Proverbs 31:10, 22-25.* **Based on this passage, is it OK for believers to wear "fine" clothes? To be involved in the fashion industry? What's the most important "clothing" here?** *Luke 3:10, 11.* **How should a Christian decide how much clothing to buy? How could you obey this teaching?** *I Peter 3:3, 4.* **Is Peter condemning nice clothes? What is he saying? How could this apply to guys *and* girls?**

Step 4
Read aloud the following list of ways to look "right." Ask whether each is OK for a Christian—and why. **(1) Making yourself throw up in order to lose weight. (2) Dyeing your hair. (3) Getting your ears pierced. (4) Having plastic surgery. (5) Taking steroids. (6) Wearing makeup. (7) Getting a tan in a booth. (8) Plucking your eyebrows. (9) Exercising for an hour a day.** In Step 5, use this simulation: **Imagine that you've been in a fire. Your face is badly disfigured. You're out of the hospital, but you'll need more skin grafts—and even then there will be major scars. How do you feel about coming back to this group? About going back to school? How do you want to be treated? How could your faith help you keep going?** Encourage kids to be thankful for the "look" they have now, and to consider the feelings of those who struggle with serious scars and disabilities.

Date Used:

Approx.
Time

Step 1: Image Is Everything _____
o Extra Action
o Small Group
o Fellowship & Worship
o Extra Fun
o Media
o Short Meeting Time
o Combined Junior High/High School
Things needed:

Step 2: First Impressions _____
o Large Group
o Mostly Guys
o Urban
Things needed:

Step 3: Friend and Creator _____
o Extra Action
o Heard It All Before
o Little Bible Background
o Mostly Girls
o Extra Challenge
Things needed:

Step 4: Obsession _____
o Mostly Girls
o Media
o Short Meeting Time
o Extra Challenge
Things needed:

Step 5: Your Own Good Looks _____
o Small Group
o Large Group
o Heard It All Before
o Little Bible Background
o Fellowship & Worship
o Mostly Guys
o Extra Fun
o Urban
o Combined Junior High/High School
Things needed:

SESSION 4

Do You Have an Attitude?

YOUR GOALS FOR THIS SESSION:

Choose one or more

☐ To help kids recognize that a person's attitude can be influenced by the people around him or her.

☐ To help kids understand that with God's help, they can maintain Christlike attitudes—especially an attitude of humility.

☐ To help kids choose to strive for good attitudes in the tough situations they face.

☐ Other _____
_____

Your Bible Base:

II Chronicles 10:1-19
Philippians 2:1-11
James 1:2-12

Word Wary

(Needed: Cut-apart copies of Repro Resource 6, timer)

Before the session, you'll need to cut apart copies of "Watch It!" (Repro Resource 6). When your group members arrive, have them form pairs. Distribute a set of cut-apart cards to each pair.

Explain: **Each card has one "guess word" on it, with five "avoid words" underneath it. As in the game Taboo, the object is to give word clues so your partner can figure out the "guess word." However, you may not use any of the "avoid words" as clues.**

Choose one person to give the clues and one person to guess. Remember—you can't say any of the "avoid words." If you do, toss that card out and go on to the next one. You have five minutes to work. I'll keep time. Ready, set, go!

When five minutes are up, ask the members of each pair to count how many words they guessed correctly. Give a round of applause to the high scorers.

Then say: **Take a minute to look at your cards again. For those of you who gave the clues, was it easy or hard for you to come up with words that weren't on the avoid list? Explain.** Have volunteers talk about what words they used to describe baseball, jeans, or any of the other "guess words."

Then ask: **For those of you who were guessing the words, do you think your partner did a good job of giving clues? Why or why not?** Get a few responses.

Then say: **This game depended a lot on the cluegiver's perception of the guess words. Some you might have felt that it was impossible not to use any of the "avoid words," so you probably had a hard time giving other clues. Others of you might have thought the game was a piece of cake and came up with a zillion clues for each word. And, in the end, your clues directly affected your partner's answers.**

STEP

2

You've Got an Attitude

(Needed: Chalkboard and chalk or newsprint and marker, three glasses of different heights, pitcher of water, table)

In the same way, a person's attitude can be directly influenced by the people around him or her—whether it's called a clique, a group, a gang, etc.

But before we talk about influences, how exactly would you define *attitude*? Give group members an opportunity to share their thoughts and definitions. Write the definitions on the board as they are given. Then use the definitions to lead into the following illustration.

Say: **To demonstrate what I mean by "attitude," let's take a look at three glasses.** Place three glasses (of different sizes) on a table. Line them up according to height, from shortest to tallest.

Then say: **The glass in the middle is between the larger and smaller glasses. To the smaller glass, the middle glass is tall. But to the larger glass, the middle one is small. It's a matter of perception.**

Fill one of the glasses about halfway full of water. Indicate the halfway mark on the glass, and say: **Would you say this glass is half empty or half full?** Take a poll of your group members to see who would say the glass is half empty and who would say it's half full.

Then explain: **If you saw a half-empty glass, you might think, "I'm almost out of water," or "Someone took a drink from my glass," or "I won't have enough to drink."**

On the other hand, if you saw a half-full glass of water, you might think, "I still have a lot left," or "I could share this with someone," or "At least it's better than if it were empty."

It all depends on how you look at it. And that's what "attitude" is—how you look at something. Think about people and things in your life. You have an attitude toward everyone and everything.

One at a time, have group members come to the board and write one- or two-word descriptions of their attitudes about school, friends, parents, studying, sports, music, dating, authority, politics, and so on. (You might want to write each category on the board, for group members to refer to.)

Afterward, read through some of the descriptions. Stop occasionally and ask: **Is this attitude positive or negative? Is it unique or is**

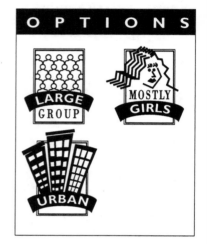

OPTIONS

LARGE GROUP

MOSTLY GIRLS

URBAN

it similar to the attitudes of many other people?

Share with your group members a negative attitude that you struggle with (hating to get up on Monday mornings, getting angry with people who tailgate, getting frustrated by slow drivers, etc.) Then have volunteers share some of the negative attitudes they struggle with.

Afterward, ask: **Why do we have these attitudes? Is it because of bad experiences we've had in the past? Is it due to the people we're with at the time? Is it due to our mood at the time?** Emphasize that there are a lot of things that influence a person's attitude.

STEP

3

Wrong-Way Rehoboam

(Needed: Bibles)

OPTIONS

EXTRA ACTION

LITTLE BIBLE BACKGROUND

SHORT MEETING TIME

JR HIGH HIGH SCHOOL COMBINED

EXTRA CHALLENGE

Have group members turn in their Bibles to II Chronicles 10. As they do so, explain that after Solomon died, his son Rehoboam succeeded him as king over Israel. As Rehoboam began his reign, the people of Israel came to him with a request.

Have volunteers take turns reading aloud verses 1-19. Afterward, say: **Rehoboam had two different attitudes toward his two groups of advisers. How would you describe his attitude toward the elders?** (He seemed to look at them as a bunch of old-timers who didn't have the guts to make the people of Israel follow his lead.)

What was Rehoboam's attitude toward the young men who had grown up with him? (He saw them as aggressive leaders who would do whatever it took to get the nation in line.)

Why do you think Rehoboam listened to his friends and adopted their attitude toward the people of Israel? (Although the passage doesn't exactly explain why, Rehoboam apparently created new positions for his friends and peers when he came to power. The king may have felt he owed his friends something. He may have also felt that the elders were OK for his father, but not for him.)

Suppose Rehoboam followed the elders' advice. Describe what his attitude toward the people might have been like. (Rehoboam would have made a wise choice in following the elders' advice. His attitude would have been one of compassion and gentleness. However, in following the advice of his friends, who had less experience in advisory positions and who were probably looking out for their own careers, Rehoboam made a foolish choice. His attitude became callous and abusive. The result was Israel's rebellion against the king.)

Explain: **The Bible gives no clear reason as to why Rehoboam had such a negative attitude toward the people of Israel. However, the Bible is pretty clear about what a Christian's attitude should be.**

STEP
4

God's Attitude Goals

(Needed: Bibles, chalkboard and chalk or newsprint and marker, pencils, copies of Repro Resource 7)

Have group members turn in their Bibles to Philippians 2:1-11. Say: **This is an "attitude" passage that's written to people who are part of God's family. I'm going to slowly read these verses. Whenever I mention an attitude, I want you to stop me and tell me what the attitude is.**

As group members call out attitudes, have a volunteer list them on the board. The list should include "tender and compassionate" "being like-minded," "having the same love," "being one in spirit and purpose," "being without selfish ambition," "not being conceited," and "humble."

Go through the list again, and ask volunteers to explain what each attitude means. Use the following ideas to supplement group members' responses.

• A *tender* and *compassionate* attitude means you care deeply about people.

• *Being like-minded, having the same love,* and *being one in spirit and purpose* emphasize unity among Christians.

• *Being without selfish ambition* involves looking out for the interests of others.

• *Not being conceited* means not thinking only of yourself.

• Being *humble* means having the right view of yourself.

Ask: **Based on this passage, what's the one basic attitude Christians should try to develop?** As group members offer their opinions, mention that verses 3 and 4 are a good summary statement of a believer's attitude: Don't do anything out of selfish ambition or vain conceit, look out for the interests of others, and have an attitude of humility.

O P T I O N S

SMALL GROUP

HEARD IT ALL BEFORE

LITTLE BIBLE BACKGROUND

MOSTLY GIRLS

MOSTLY GUYS

EXTRA FUN

MEDIA

URBAN

JR. HIGH HIGH SCHOOL COMBINED

Say: **Humility probably doesn't appear on too many people's top ten lists of attitudes. How would you describe the basic attitude of many people today?** (Assertive, demanding their personal rights, looking out for themselves, looking for ways to become successful and get ahead.)

Yet humility seems to be a key attitude. It's the attitude Rehoboam should have had, and it's the attitude Jesus did have when He gave up the glory of heaven to come to earth as a man.

Being humble doesn't mean being a nonassertive, "door-mat" kind of person. It does mean, however, that you aren't proud or boastful. If you have an attitude of humility, you have a proper mind-set about who you are. Humility also promotes helpfulness, generosity, and gratitude.

Have someone read aloud James 1:2-12. Then make another list on the board of the attitudes James describes. Joyfulness, perseverance, and humility are the key attitudes you're looking for.

Explain: **In Philippians, Paul talks about an overall attitude of humility and Christlikeness. Here, James talks about our attitudes in one specific situation—going through trials.**

According to James, what kind of attitude should we have when trials come our way? (Believe it or not, James says to consider it "pure joy" when we face trials.)

What's your honest reaction to James's instruction? (Is he crazy or what?)

Explain: **James was a big picture kind of guy. From his perspective, hard times developed perseverance—the ability to tough it out and not give up—and perseverance developed a mature faith that wouldn't collapse at the first sign of trouble. In the end, the believer who withstands the test will receive a crown of life.**

Hand out copies of "The Be-Joyful Attitudes" (Repro Resource 7) and pencils. Explain: **Read through each of the situations on the sheet and the factors that might influence each situation. Then write down a response for each one that demonstrates a Christlike attitude.**

Give group members a few minutes to complete the sheet. When they're finished, ask volunteers to share what they wrote. Encourage the volunteers to explain how they could handle the influences and still maintain a Christlike attitude in each situation.

Attitude Check

(Needed: Bibles)

Summarize: **As we wrap up this session, think about a specific attitude that you struggle with. Or think of a tough situation that you went through and had a pretty hard time with. Or think of a situation in which God helped you maintain a positive attitude.**

If group members want to, let them express their feelings about the situations and perhaps even share prayer requests about problem areas. Those who don't want to share should just silently consider the situations.

Read aloud Philippians 2:5-7 and James 1:2, 3. Encourage group members to read, and even try to memorize, these verses during the week.

Then close the session in prayer, asking God to help your group members develop and maintain positive, Christlike attitudes.

O P T I O N S

FELLOWSHIP &
WORSHIP

WATCH IT!

BASEBALL
game
stadium
play
bat
pitcher

BLACKTOP
asphalt
driveway
parking
pavement
cement

HORSESHOE
hoof
nail
blacksmith
game
backyard

PLAYPEN
baby
crib
toys
portable
sleep

JEANS
denim
stonewashed
bleach
blue
Levis

GLOVES
mittens
winter
hands
warm
garden

PIZZA
crust
cheese
pepperoni
sausage
deliver

INSECT
bug
fly
spider
mosquito
exterminator

CALENDAR
month
day
year
week
date

ANSWERING MACHINE
automatic
telephone
message
leave
time

The Be-Joyful ATTITUDES

SITUATION #1

At last, the weekend has arrived! But as you walk in the door, your brother hands you the phone. Your friend from history class announces that you've got to do all the research for next week's project because he has to visit his aunt this weekend.

Influences—You already have an essay to write for English, an experiment for science, and a test in trig to prepare for.

Your response:

SITUATION #2

Your gym teacher tells the class that he's decided to have the mile run today instead of the day after tomorrow. A large portion of your grade depends on your performance.

Influences—You didn't feel well last night after dinner, and really didn't get a good night's sleep.

Your response:

SITUATION #3

Your boss has to leave early from work. He hands you the keys and says to clean up and lock the front door when you leave.

Influences—At any moment your friends are going to show up. You're supposed to go with them to grab a bite to eat.

Your response:

SITUATION #4

You and your friends want to see the new action movie that everyone's raving about, but one of your friends is running late and you barely make it to the theater on time. You drop your friends off at the box office, park the car, and run to meet them—all for nothing. The show has been sold out.

Influences—This is probably the last weekend the movie will be at your local theater.

Your response:

SITUATION #5

Your track coach lets you know that you will be the alternate in the track meet tomorrow against the cross-town rivals.

Influences—You've been practicing late every day this week and were geared up for a rematch against the guy who beat you last time.

Your response:

EXTRA ACTION

Step 1

Replace Steps 1 and 2 with a new opener. Before the session, write the following attitudes on separate index cards: "I'm so cool"; "Angry"; "Don't hurt me"; "Too busy"; "Suspicious"; "Depressed"; "Have a nice day." Make two sets of cards, each in a different order. have group members form teams. Give each team a stack of cards. The first person on each team will draw a card, and then walk to the opposite wall and back in a way that reflects the attitude on the card. Other team members must guess the attitude before the next person goes. The first team to get through its cards wins. Then ask kids to demonstrate how they'd walk in the following situations, and what attitudes their walks would reflect. **(1) You're going to the principal's office, knowing you're in trouble. (2) You're going to the platform at graduation to make a speech. (3) You're on your way to church. Ask: What does it mean when someone "has an attitude"? How would you describe your overall attitude?**

Step 3

Skip Step 3. In Step 4, have group members form teams of three. As you read the passage aloud, whenever you come to an attitude, each team should form a "living sculpture" to demonstrate it. Take a Polaroid photo of the first (or best) sculpture for each attitude. Display the photos on the wall as a reminder. Skip Repro Resource 7 for now. In Step 5, give each "living sculpture" team a situation cut from Repro Resource 7. Have one person act out a Christlike response and the other two, representing the "Influences," try to drag him or her off the "stage." Discuss the fact that the right attitudes don't just appear; we get them by wanting to be Christlike, by letting God's Spirit change us, and by practicing.

SMALL GROUP

Step 1

Want a more direct introduction to the topic? Replace Steps 1 and 2 with a new opener tailored to a small group. Bring an eye patch for each person—either the kind sold in pharmacies or the kind you can make from elastic and construction paper. Have kids wear the eye patches as they try to accomplish the following the feats: reach out and touch someone else's nose; walk toward a wall without running into it; play Ping-Pong or catch. Afterward, ask kids how they did. Most will have had trouble; using one eye allows only two-dimensional vision, making it hard to judge distances. Talk about *attitude* as the way we see things. Ask: **What ways of seeing things are thought to be cool right now? How are those ways of seeing things limited? What kinds of experiences might give a person "two-dimensional" attitudes?**

Step 4

A large group might split up the Repro Resource situations to cover them in less time; if that's not possible for you, try another approach. Choose just two of the situations. Ask how people with the following attitudes might react to them: "I'm mad at the world"; "I have to do everything perfectly"; "God hates me"; and "I can't do anything right." Ask: **What might be the results of these reactions?** Then discuss what a Christlike reaction might be in the two situations.

LARGE GROUP

Step 1

For a more direct and involving introduction to the topic, try this: Bring a tape player and a variety of recorded music. Include music reflecting various attitudes— boastful or angry rap, worshipful or contrite contemporary Christian music, defiant heavy metal, self-absorbed pop, sad or cynical country, etc. Play parts of songs, changing tapes frequently. Whenever you stop the tape, kids must strike a pose reflecting the attitude they hear in the music (fist raised to show rebellion, strutting to show pride, etc.) Then ask kids to list attitudes that are usually associated with various styles of music and clothes. Ask: **Do people get their attitudes from music and clothes, or do they choose music and clothes because they have certain attitudes? Explain.**

Step 2

Use the step as written, but with a more involving twist. Prepare four kinds of slips that say the following: (1) "You think all authority figures are jerks. Ridicule what the leader does." (2) "You think life is a big joke. Try to get the attention of those around you by being funny." (3) "You think anyone who doesn't follow the rules is disgusting. Complain about those who aren't paying attention." (4) "You have great respect for the leader. Do your best to hear every word the leader says." Copy the slips so that each person can have one. Pass them out at the beginning of the step, distributing approximately equal numbers of each kind. Kids should do as the slips say during your object lesson with the water glasses. Afterward, call a halt to the chaos, discuss what happened and the attitudes that caused it, and finish the step.

Step 1
Bring two boxes of crayons. Unwrap each crayon and replace it in its box. Have group members form two teams. Give each team a box of crayons. Tell Team A: **You feel great. You just aced the driver's test and were asked out by the person of your dreams.** Tell Team B: **You feel lousy. You just flunked the driver's test and were turned down for a date with the person of your dreams.** Tell both teams: **Come up with names for the colors of these crayons—names that reflect your feelings.** Chances are you'll hear names like "emerald green" from Team A and names like "puke green" from Team B. Use this to illustrate the way our attitudes affect everything we do. In Step 2, use something fresher than the water glass analogy. Look up the word *attitude* in the dictionary. Note the definition related to spacecraft and aircraft; attitude is your position in relation to a fixed point. Ask: **What fixed point can we use to figure out what a "good attitude" is?** Skip Step 3.

Step 4
Kids may think, "I don't *feel* these attitudes. Why pretend that I do?" Ask kids to sit in a variety of poses (defiantly crossing their arms, leaning back in boredom, etc.). Have them say things that *don't* go with their body language. (Example: Saying "I really care about that" while shrugging.) Ask: **Is this what the Bible means? Are we supposed to force ourselves to have Christlike attitudes no matter how we feel?** Read Ephesians 4:22-24. Point out that changing our attitudes involves changing our minds to match the new "selves" given to us when we become Christians. We may not have the right attitudes to start with, but if we don't at least *want* the right attitudes, we need to ask ourselves whether we really belong to Christ.

Step 3
Replace the Rehoboam study with more accessible passages about "bad attitudes." Read Proverbs 6:9-11. Ask: **What attitude is described here? How have you seen it in action?** Read Proverbs 6:16-19. Ask: **Which of these attitudes are popular in movies? In music? At school? Why do you think God hates them?** Read Proverbs 6:32. Ask: **What attitudes about sex do kids in your school have? What would they think of this verse?** Read Luke 12:16-21. Ask: **Is this attitude more popular among kids or adults? Explain. What's the opposite of this attitude?** Read Romans 13:1, 2. Ask: **Would life be more fun or less fun if everyone obeyed these verses? Why? What do you think most kids' attitude toward authority is?**

Step 4
Kids may wonder, "Are Christians supposed to be robots? Can't I ever be mad about what people do to me or the 'trials' I go through?" Show how Jesus handled these issues. Read about how hard it was for Jesus to give up His life (Matthew 26:36-46; Luke 22:42-44). He didn't squelch His feelings, yet He made a decision to do the right thing despite His feelings—because He wanted to obey God and knew what the results of His obedience would be (Hebrews 12:1-3). Affirm that Christians are supposed to have feelings too. But we have a choice: to let tough times dictate what our attitudes will be, or to have attitudes that help us cope with tough times.

Step 1
Have kids form small groups. Call out a day of the week and an hour (Tuesday at 4 p.m., Sunday at 9 a.m., etc.). Members of each small group should tell each other what their attitude usually is at that time, and why. (Examples: "I'm at football practice, so I'm ready to break some bones"; "I'm on the way to church, feeling hassled because we're in a big hurry.") Then call out a place (Pizza Hut, a pep rally); group members should tell each other how they usually feel there and why. Do this once or twice more if time allows.

Step 5
Have kids try the following postures, all with eyes closed: standing with heads bowed; standing with arms outstretched, face toward the sky; sitting with head bowed; sitting casually, legs crossed; kneeling; bowing down with head touching the floor. Ask: **How might each of these positions affect your attitude if you used it when you prayed? What are some advantages and disadvantages of each? Which do you think would work best for you? Why?** Sing one or more songs that express an attitude ("Alleluia," "Rejoice in the Lord Always," etc.). Then, if you think kids will take it seriously, let each person pray in the position of his or her choice.

MOSTLY GIRLS

Step 2

After using the glasses of water to demonstrate attitude, ask: **Do you think people you know have primarily a positive attitude or a negative attitude? Explain.** Ask each group member to write down the names of ten people who are a part of her life on a regular basis, including people of all ages. Then ask group members to make a mark beside each name to indicate whether that person is more positive about everyday events or negative about them. Discuss how we are influenced by those around us, and what to do when we live with many negative influences.

Step 4

Ask group members to discuss the difference between a mood and an attitude. Say: **Unfortunately, girls are often known for their moods. How do you respond to someone who says, "If I'm having a bad day, I'm not really responsible for my attitude"? When you have a bad attitude about something and realize that it is wrong, how can you change it?**

MOSTLY GUYS

Step 1

Replace Steps 1 and 2 with a guy-tailored opener. Play clips from three or four stand-up comics' performances that you've taped from TV or rented on video. Try for a variety of attitudes: one cynical (like Dennis Miller), one depressed (like Stephen Wright), one goofy (like Steve Martin), one frustrated (like Jerry Seinfeld). Discuss the attitudes of these comics and the attitudes their audiences are likely to pick up. Ask: **What other attitudes can come across in comedy?** (Putting down women and people of other races; being "cooler than thou"; anger; good-natured fun; swearing is funny; etc.) **What attitudes do we pick up from male characters on TV and in movies? From our friends?**

Step 4

Why would a guy want to be tender, compassionate, unambitious, and humble? Look at passages that show Jesus being tough (Matthew 27:34), critical (Matthew 23:33, 34), forceful (Mark 11:15-17), ambitious (John 12:31, 32), and assertive (Luke 4:28-30). Note that Jesus did these things without being selfish. Being tender *and* tough, compassionate *and* critical, etc., are signs of being a *complete* man—not a weak one.

EXTRA FUN

Step 1

Have group members form pairs. Give each pair a dozen Pringles potato chips (to ensure equal size of chips). Partners will stand face-to-face. Each partner will place a chip on each shoulder of the other. Partners must eat the chips off their own shoulders, repeating the process until all chips are gone. Any pair that drops a chip is out. No one can place chips on his or her own shoulders. The first pair to eat all of its chips wins. Tie this into having "a chip on your shoulder," an attitude a lot of people seem to have these days.

Step 4

Play "Force Field." Have kids stand at random throughout the room. You will call out the name of a group member, who instantly has a "force field" (ten feet in diameter) around him or her. The person with the force field can move anywhere in the room; other kids must stay at least five feet away from him or her (you be the judge, estimating visually), or they're out. Then, without warning, call out the name of another player who now has the force field. Give kids no more than ten seconds to keep their distance from the new "force field generator." Call out new names as often as you wish, sending kids scrambling. Anyone still in the game after three minutes gets a prize. Point out that many people put on tough or aloof attitudes to keep others away, to keep from being hurt. But the only attitude that really helps us cope with hurt is the one in James 1:2-12.

Step 1

Play a recorded rock song. Have kids write "reviews" of the song. The catch is that each person is trying to impress someone with his or her review. For one person it may be the lead singer; for another, a former English teacher; for others, the backup singers, the drummer, the lead guitarist, the youth leader, or a parent. Read the results. See whether kids can guess who the writers were trying to impress. Then note that we often "put on" an attitude to try to impress or intimidate someone else. Ask: **Does putting on an attitude really impress people? Why or why not?**

Step 4

Show a couple of scenes of conflict from a TV show you've taped. Discuss each character's attitude in the scene. Ask: **What might each scene have been like if the characters had Christlike attitudes?** Note that since most TV shows tell stories, and stories require conflict, viewers are bombarded with people fighting and insulting each other. A lot of people come to think that's normal behavior. Ask: **Can you think of any ways to avoid picking up these attitudes?**

Step 1

Replace Steps 1 and 2 with a shorter opener. Seat kids in a circle. Have each person finish this sentence: **When I look at the sunset, I see . . .** Every couple of kids or so, call out a way in which the next person must modify his or her answer in comparison to the previous one (crabbier, warmer, colder, more scientific, more depressed, happier, more full of wonder, more sarcastic, more angry, more confused, more polite, etc.). Anyone who can't come up with an appropriate response in five seconds is out. If time allows, try it again with this sentence: **The cooks in the school cafeteria are . . .** Discuss how our attitudes affect the way we see things—and even the way *others* see things.

Step 3

Skip Step 3. In Step 4, use just the first three situations on Repro Resource 7. In Step 5, let kids choose either #4 or #5 from the Repro Resource. Have them write what their responses would *really* be at this point, and compare them to what they think Jesus might do. Share results as time allows.

Step 2

People are influenced heavily by the groups they hang around with. To prove this point, split your group into two teams. One team will be the "negative view," and the other will be the "positive view." You will give three urban community issues for each team to debate according to its disposition, in an attempt to top the opposing point of the other team. Any team that cannot come up with a counterpoint in ten seconds loses. Give five minutes for each team to gather its thoughts (on each separate issue). Consider using these three issues: (1) Can we get rid of the drug problem? (2) Are there enough role models for children? (3) Does the welfare system help people? Afterward, assuming emotions have been stirred in defense of the teams' positions, discuss how easy it is to be influenced by a group so strongly that an individual no longer questions whether the group is doing right.

Step 4

You may want to add the following situation to Repro 7.
Situation #6
While you're riding the bus home from school with your friends, two white boys get on one stop before you get off. Your friends say to you, "We hate whites—let's beat them up when they get off."
Influences—Your parents said you will be grounded if you don't come straight home, since you've been late for the past three days. But if you get off to go home, those white boys will surely get hurt. What will your response be?

Step 3

The Rehoboam story may be hard for kids to relate to their own attitudes. Skip it. Have kids stand in a circle, with an empty chair in the middle. Say: **I'm going to read a list of people and things that we'll imagine are sitting in that chair. After each one, move forward or backward to show how close you'd want to be to that person or thing. Here's the list: a box of free candy bars, a nuclear bomb, your best friend, your favorite movie star, a homeless person, someone who stole your lunch money when you were little, your grandmother, a gang leader, a blind person.** Afterward, discuss the attitudes kids displayed. Ask: **Which of these attitudes do you think please God? Which probably don't? Which do you think He doesn't care about?**

Step 4

Most of the situations on Repro Resource 7 are more typical of high school than junior high. Here are two situations to substitute: **(1) You trade one of your best baseball cards for three cards a friend owns. Moments later, your friend accidentally spills ketchup on the cards you just got, lowering their value. Influence—This is not your best friend. (2) You're baby-sitting. Just as the parents leave, the mom says, "Oh, please get little Andrew to take his vitamins and pick up his toys. We couldn't get him to." Influences—Andrew is often a little monster, and the parents never pay you extra for such chores.** In Step 5, make the application more concrete. Ask kids to name someone they think is cool. How would that person handle the situations you just discussed? Observe that if those responses aren't Christlike, kids may need to redefine what's cool. Encourage them to see Jesus as *the* example of having the right attitude.

Step 1

Replace Steps 1 and 2 with a new opener. Read the following quotes and ask kids to tell you what attitudes they reflect. **(1) "Love is what happens to a man and a woman who don't know each other"** (W. Somerset Maugham). **(2) "Everyone is special, each of us in his or her own way"** (Barney the Dinosaur). **(3) "God is love, but get it in writing"** (Gypsy Rose Lee). **(4) "What was that chick's name?"** (Geraldo Rivera). **(5) "He who laughs has not yet heard the bad news"** (Bertolt Brecht). **(6) "I'm too big; I'm too dumb; I'm too clumsy"** (David Letterman). **(7) "Surely goodness and love will follow me all the days of my life"** (David in Psalm 23:6). Then ask: **Which of these attitudes do you see most at school? Which is most like your attitude toward life?**

Step 3

Skip the II Chronicles study. Ask: **How might these childhood experiences shape a person's attitudes: seeing your parents divorce, getting straight As without having to work at it, being held back a grade, being sexually abused, losing an older brother, having great times in a church club program, being teased about your weight?** Read about Joseph and his brothers (Genesis 37:3-8, 23-27; 39:1, 2; 41:53; 42:1-3, 6-8; 45:1-7, 12-15). Ask: **How were the attitudes of Joseph and his brothers toward each other shaped by their experiences? How were their reactions different? Why?** Note that we don't have to be slaves to our bad experiences. With God's help, and sometimes the aid of human counselors, we can form healthy attitudes despite traumas. Ask: **Do you have trouble with someone else's "bad attitude"? What kind of experiences might have led to that attitude?**

Date Used:

Approx.
Time

Step 1: Word Wary _____
o Extra Action
o Small Group
o Large Group
o Heard It All Before
o Fellowship & Worship
o Mostly Guys
o Extra Fun
o Media
o Short Meeting Time
o Extra Challenge
Things needed:

Step 2: You've Got an Attitude _____
o Large Group
o Mostly Girls
o Urban
Things needed:

Step 3: Wrong-Way Rehoboam _____
o Extra Action
o Little Bible Background
o Short Meeting Time
o Combined Junior High/High School
o Extra Challenge
Things needed:

Step 4: God's Attitude Goals _____
o Small Group
o Heard It All Before
o Little Bible Background
o Mostly Girls
o Mostly Guys
o Extra Fun
o Media
o Urban
o Combined Junior High/High School
Things needed:

Step 5: Attitude Check _____
o Fellowship & Worship
Things needed:

Getting Along with Other People's Styles

YOUR GOALS FOR THIS SESSION:

Choose one or more

☐ To help kids recognize that James and other Jewish leaders of the early church welcomed the Gentiles as believers and accepted the differences in background and style.

☐ To help kids understand what it means that all people were created in God's image.

☐ To help kids develop wise judgment when dealing with people who have different styles than they have.

☐ Other _____

Your Bible Base:

Matthew 7:1-5
Acts 15:1-41
James 2:1-13

Buddy, Can You Spare a Hand?

(Needed: Several pairs of untied shoes)

As group members arrive, give each one an untied shoe. Explain: **I want you to tie this shoe using only one hand. You have to hold your other hand behind your back.**

Give group members a few minutes to figure out how to tie their shoes. You might offer a few "helpful" suggestions, but the task should be nearly impossible to complete. Pay attention to the way group members try to tie their shoes. Call time before everyone reaches the point of total frustration.

Then say: **Let's try this again, but this time with a partner.** Have group members pair up and work together to tie one of the shoes. Again, each person may only use one hand; the other hand must be kept behind his or her back.

Give the pairs a few minutes to work; then call "Time." Congratulate any pairs that accomplish the task.

Say: **We all know how to tie our shoes, but doing it one-handed it is nearly impossible. Was it any easier with a partner? After all, you did have two hands.** Give group members a chance to voice their frustrations with or appreciation of their partners.

When you were working together, what was the hardest thing to overcome? Let group members share their feelings. Some pairs may have had two left-handed people working together, or two righties. Some pairs may have experienced poor communication. Other pairs may have been faced with trying to make two different shoe-tying methods work together.

Summarize: **Probably the biggest problems you had were ones that neither you nor your partner had any control over—things like being left-handed, or having learned different shoe-tying methods. It's pretty hard to change these kinds of things when you've been doing them a certain way for so long.**

These same types of differences, whether they're ingrained or inborn, can make getting along with other people just as frustrating as trying to tie a shoe with one hand behind your back.

Taking Stock of Us and Them

(Needed: Pencils, copies of Repro Resource 8)

Say: **In this series, we've been talking about our personal styles and what it means to have a personal style.** Briefly mention the previous sessions on style, music, looks, and attitudes. **Everyone has a different style; and when styles collide, problems arise.**

Pass out copies of "Your Social Survey" (Repro Resource 8) and pencils. Say: **Let's examine how much contact you have with people who may have totally different styles than you have. You might be surprised at how often you deal with someone else's style.**

Give group members a few minutes to complete the sheet. When they're finished, ask volunteers to estimate how often they deal with other people's styles.

Say: **If it were left up to most of us, we'd probably choose to be with only the people we like best and get along with. But sometimes it's not up to us, and that's when personal styles can create tension.**

Think of a specific time this past week in which you had to deal with someone whose style was either slightly different than yours or radically opposite of the way you do things. Give group members a few minutes to think. If possible, share an experience of your own, and then give group members a chance to share. Point out that potential style collisions might occur while working together on school projects, while doing a presentation together, during sports activities, etc.

After someone shares an experience, ask: **How did you feel about the way you handled the situation?** Encourage group members to talk honestly about their reactions and the specific things they did to cope (or not cope) with the differences.

Then say: **The Bible gives a good example of how to deal with someone who has a different style from our own.**

O P T I O N S

EXTRA ACTION

LARGE GROUP

MEDIA

URBAN

STEP 3

Harmony and Disharmony

(Needed: Bibles)

OPTIONS

EXTRA ACTION

SMALL GROUP

HEARD IT ALL BEFORE

LITTLE BIBLE BACKGROUND

MOSTLY GIRLS

MEDIA

SHORT MEETING TIME

URBAN

JR.HIGH HIGH SCHOOL COMBINED

Have your group members turn in their Bibles to Acts 15. As they do, give them some background on the story. Explain that Paul and Barnabas had returned from their first missionary journey to the church at Antioch, which was north of present-day Israel (Acts 14:26-28). Some men, probably "the party of Pharisees" (which seemed to include some believers) mentioned in Acts 15:5, had come to Antioch and were teaching that believers had to be circumcised to be saved. To correct this teaching, Paul and Barnabas and other church leaders went to Jerusalem to meet with the church there.

Have someone read aloud verses 1-5. Then ask: **What was the issue that was being discussed and debated?** (The issue was whether or not Gentile believers had to be circumcised and required to obey the law of Moses.)

Point out that the differences bewteen the Jews and Gentiles had escalated over the centuries into full-blown hatred and prejudice. And these two groups were now being asked to come together and become one in Christ.

Have someone read aloud verses 6-12. Then say: **Peter clearly defended the Gentiles. How did he back up his point?** (Peter said that he was chosen by God to preach specifically to the Gentiles. God showed that *He* accepted the Gentiles by giving them the Holy Spirit just as He had to the Jews.)

What do you think was Peter's strongest argument for accepting the Gentiles as they were? (God had accepted the Gentiles without circumcision or the law of Moses. Peter's statement in Acts 15:11 sums up the argument: "It is through the grace of our Lord Jesus that we are saved, *just as they are!*" [italics added].)

What did Barnabas and Paul add to the discussion? (They related their experiences on their missionary journey into the Gentile provinces of Asia.)

Why do you think Peter, Paul, and Barnabas defended the Gentile believers? (They wanted to correct wrong thinking about salvation. They also had spent time with the Gentiles and had gotten to know them and discovered how much they loved the Lord.)

Have someone read aloud verses 13-21. Then say: **James brings another authority into the picture. God's very Word de-**

clares that God has chosen Gentiles to bear His name. And who's to argue with God's Word? James then gives his full support to accepting the Gentiles.

What are James's suggestions for resolving the differences? (Instead of making things difficult for the Gentiles who are turning to God, the Jewish believers should write a letter to the Gentile believers with these four stipulations: abstain from food polluted by idols, abstain from sexual immorality, abstain from the meat of strangled animals, and abstain from blood.)

You'll probably need to explain why James wanted these stipulations. The culture of that time was hevily influenced by pagan worship practices. These practices were especially prevalent among Gentiles and were especially repulsive to Jews (because they violated God's laws).

Explain: **From James's perspective, it would help the relationships between the Gentiles and Jews if these requirements were kept.**

Do you think James was being unreasonable? Why or why not? (James's solution was a good way to resolve the differences and encourage good relationships. James wasn't asking the Gentiles to give up their identities and become just like the Jewish believers. He was asking the Gentiles to give up practices that were associated with a godless culture—and in doing so, they would promote harmony.)

Have someone read aloud verses 22-35. Then ask: **What was the final outcome?** (The church at Antioch gave advice and encouragement to the Gentile believers, who were glad and strengthened in their faith. The results were positive, as the two groups spent time trying to understand the differences between them.)

Have someone read aloud verses 36-41. Then ask: **What's the difference in style here?** (Barnabas and Paul differ in who they choose for traveling companions. They differ so much that they part company and go their separate ways.)

What do you think of the solution to their problem? Was it right? Was it wrong? Explain. Ask several group members to offer their opinions. Encourage them to put themselves in Paul's and Barnabas's shoes. Remind them of the purpose of the missionary journeys—to spread the good news of the Gospel, not to travel with a particular person.

Summarize: **In the long run, the parting of ways was the right choice. Both teams went ahead in their ministries and were very effective. From what Paul wrote in later letters in the New Testament, he came to respect Mark.**

Remember, different isn't wrong. As long as you can live with someone else's style, you don't always have to resolve the differences between you.

STEP 4

Here Comes the Judge

(Needed: Bibles, pencils, copies of Repro Resource 9)

Pass out copies of "You Make the Call" (Repro Resource 9). Instruct group members to read through the scenarios and write down their solutions on the back of the sheet.

Give group members a few minutes to work. When they're finished, go through the situations one at a time and have volunteers share their solutions.

Then say: **OK, we've come up with some solutions based on our personal opinions. Now let's come up with some solutions based on God's Word.**

Have group members form two teams. Instruct Team 1 to look up Matthew 7:1-5 and apply the principles of the passage to Situations 1 and 3. Instruct Team 2 to look up James 2:1-13 and apply the principles of the passage to Situations 2 and 4.

As group members work, make sure they understand what the passages are saying. For the Matthew passage, point out that Christ is condemning the hypocritical, self-righteous kind of judging. For the James passage, James bluntly condemns favoritism.

As group members work in their teams, have them compare the solutions they wrote down earlier with the biblical principles they find in their assigned passages. Do they need to come up with different solutions, based on God's principles?

After a few minutes, have each team share its findings. Use the following information to supplement the teams' responses.

• *Situation 1*—Kurt judged Mark's taste in music. In essence, he belittled Mark because of his musical preference. According to Matthew 7:1-5, Kurt has no right to do that. In doing so, Kurt sets himself up to be judged according to the same standards.

• *Situation 2*—Sean is wrong for judging Otis by his appearance. And his suggestion that Kristie ask Otis to leave demonstrates that Sean believes he's better than Otis. But he isn't. Kristie should refrain from showing favoritism and ignore Sean's request.

• *Situation 3*—Karen certainly has no right to *judge* Angie on the basis of her driving habits. After all, Karen does the exact same things when she drives. But Karen does have the right to point out the dangers of Angie's driving habits—as long as she recognizes her own faults in the same areas.

• *Situation 4*—Ken has no right to judge the new guys based on their abilities. He should welcome them to the team.

If you have time, ask volunteers to share some experiences they've had in which they had to deal with favoritism, a lack of acceptance, or being judged. If possible, share an experience of your own to get things started.

The Finishing Touch

Have group members close their eyes and think of people in their lives whom they tend to shy away from just because these people are different. Then ask the following questions, allowing plenty of time between questions for group members to think about their responses.

Why do you shy away from this person?

Are you ever rude to this person?

How is he or she different from you?

Is there a good reason you should steer clear of this person?

Have you spent any time getting to know him or her?

Have you made an offer of friendship to this person?

Is there something you could do tomorrow that would communicate friendliness and care to this person?

How would Jesus have treated this person?

Is it possible for you to treat him or her the same way?

Have group members keep their eyes closed for prayer. Thank God for the group of individuals He's brought together in your group. Thank Him for their different interests and styles. Ask God to help them let Him shape their attitudes of themselves and others. Finally, thank Him for the example that Christ set for His people to follow.

YOUR SOCIAL SURVEY

For each of the following questions, put a check mark in the box that best answers that question.

	NEVER	SOMETIMES	OFTEN	ALWAYS
1. How often do you see your next-door neighbors?				
2. How often do you try to get to know personally the salespeople who call your house?				
3. How often do you have disagreements with someone in your family?				
4. How often do you get to sit next to your best friend in school?				
5. At family gatherings, how often do you get stuck talking to relatives you have nothing in common with?				
6. How often do you *really* pay attention to your least favorite teacher in school?				
7. How often do you talk to the people in line with you at the store?				
8. How often do you have to babysit your younger brother or sister (or someone else younger than you)?				
9. How often do you get assigned school projects with people you don't know very well?				
10. How often are you put in a situation in which you have to talk with someone you've never met before?				

You Make the CALL

1. Mark and Kurt have been best friends all their lives. They both learned to play the trumpet in fourth grade. They both made the orchestra at school on their first try. They both taught themselves to play the guitar as freshmen. And they've never missed a local concert.

Then one Thursday Kurt called Mark.

"Mark, guess what? I've got two tickets for the concert Friday night! And my parents said I could go. Do you think you can..."

"Whoa! Hang on," Mark jumped in. "I've got two tickets to the other concert Friday night."

"You mean for that—I almost can't say it—that country band?"

"Yeah, what's wrong with that?"

"I can't stand that twangy, whining excuse for music!" Kurt complained.

"Look, I'm not going to your concert," Mark said.

"And I'm not going to yours!" Kurt replied.

Who's right? Who's wrong? What do these guys need to do?

2. Kristie has invited her church youth group over for a Christmas party. Everybody shows up dressed for the occasion, all smiles and full of yuletide spirit.

Everyone except Otis, that is. He's been to only one group meeting before, and no one really knows him. He's quiet and aloof. He also isn't dressed up like everyone else.

At the punch bowl, Sean comes over to Kristie.

"Why don't you have Otis go home. He's a real downer for the party. People are starting to feel sorry for him. They're not enjoying themselves."

"I can't do that," Kristie replies.

"Well, then maybe the rest of us will leave." Sean takes his punch and walks away.

What should Kristie do? As hostess, she's responsible for making everybody feel welcome. And she certainly doesn't want *anyone* to leave.

3. It's Friday. School's out. Karen wants to get home. She drives out of the school parking lot, forgetting to signal. She speeds through an intersection just as the light changes to red. She races over railroad tracks, ignoring the 35 m.p.h. speed limit. She also doesn't yield for a pedestrian on the street.

Later that afternoon, Karen's mom asks Karen to take her younger sister Angie out driving. Angie just got her license.

Guess what? Angie doesn't signal. She doesn't yield. She goes over the speed limit. She doesn't even notice stoplights changing to red.

Karen has just about had it. Angie is driving recklessly. As an older sister, Karen's got to say something. But can she? Should she?

4. The church softball team is getting ready for its first game of the season. As Ken gathers all the guys together for practice, the youth pastor drives up with another bunch of guys. He introduces them; they're the exchange students from Eastern Europe, and they want to join the team.

Now last year, the team made it to the league tournament and almost won the championship game. Ken is convinced that the team now has the experience to go all the way.

But these new guys don't know softball. They can barely speak English. How can they be of any help to the team?

The youth pastor comes over to Ken and asks if they can join the team.

What should Ken say? How will his team be affected?

Step 2

Instead of having kids fill out Repro Resource 8, adapt it as follows. Have kids stand arm's length apart. They should face you or turn away from you as you read the following greetings. The degree to which they turn away from you should show how much their styles usually clash with the kind of person who's greeting them. The greetings are as follows: **(1) Howdy, neighbor! (2) Hi, I'm calling from AT&G Long Distance; how are you this evening? (3) This is your father speaking. (4) Dear, it's your mother. (5) Why, it's my favorite nephew (niece)! Look how you've grown! (6) Good morning, class. Here's your English test. (7) All right, take three laps and hit the showers! (8) Hi, I'm your new locker (or lab) partner.**

Step 3

While discussing Acts 15:1-35, let only half of the group (representing the Pharisees) have Bibles. But accept answers only from those who *don't* have Bibles (representing the Gentiles). Each group will sit on opposite sides of the room. "Pharisees" must look up the verses; "Gentiles" must cross the room and have the verses explained to them by the "Pharisees" before answering. Use this as an illustration of the chasm that existed between the two groups. In Step 4, instead of having kids read the situations on the sheet, have a pair of kids (situations 1 and 3) and the whole group (situations 2 and 4) panto-mime the stories as you read them. Let kids call out possible solutions instead of writing them.

Step 3

Lengthy interrogation on a lengthy passage is intimidating when a few kids have to answer all the questions. Skip Acts 15. Have group members form two teams. Assign Team A to read John 12:1-8. Ask: **What problem did Mary's style cause? How do you react to people who do emotional, "weird" things in church? How did Jesus react?** Assign Team B to read Luke 18:35-43. Ask: **What problem did the blind man's style cause? How do you react to people who are loud, insistent, or have bad manners? How did Jesus react?** Have the whole group read Ephesians 4:2-6; 5:19-21. Ask: **What styles are hardest for you to "bear with"? What efforts have you made to keep this group together despite differences? What efforts could you make? Why should we submit to one another? If we did, what might be the overall "style" of our group?**

Step 5

Deal with the challenge of getting along in a small group. Have kids crowd together as closely as possible and stare at each other. The first person to smile or laugh has to complete this sentence: **The best thing about being in a small group is . . .** The second person to smile or laugh must finish this sentence: **The worst thing about being in a small group is . . .** Talk about how it's easy to see our differences in style when we're in a small group. Ask: **How are we dealing with that?** Then have kids spread out as far from each other as they can. Have volunteers finish this sentence: **If people with a different style from mine tried to join this group, I would . . .** Finally, have group members sit at a normal distance from each other. Encourage kids not to make the group smaller than it is by letting style differences keep group members apart.

Step 2

Reporting survey answers could take a long time. Instead, designate the four corners of the room as "Never," "Sometimes," "Often," and "All the Time." Read the survey questions aloud; after each, have kids move to the appropriate corners to indicate answers. In Step 3, break the question-and-answer routine. While kids are looking up answers to the second discussion question, two or three kids (whom you've prepared beforehand) should stage a fight over which Bible translation to use. Each actor should explain loudly why his or her Bible's style is best, leading to a shoving match and chasing each other out of the room. After the actors return, ask the group: **How was this fight like the one in Acts 15? How could it be resolved?**

Step 5

Deal with getting along in a large group. Before the session, take two inexpensive cardboard jigsaw puzzles and cut all the tabs (the parts that stick out) from the pieces. Throw the tabs away and return the pieces to their boxes. At this point in the meeting, have group members form two teams. Give each team a puzzle. Announce that the team that puts its puzzle together first will win. Kids should discover very quickly that the pieces won't fit. Explain that you figured the puzzles would fit better if rough edges and parts that "stuck out like a sore thumb" were removed. Tie this into the group's need for people with all sorts of styles—even those we think have rough edges or who "stick out like a sore thumb." Note how easy it is in a large group to avoid people with other styles. Then have the whole group stand in a circle and move into the eyes-closed exercise in the basic session plan—each person applying it specifically to another in your group.

Step 3

Do your kids know they aren't supposed to *fight* over conflicting styles, but think it's OK to *put down* people who are different? Skip Acts 15. Pass around several satirical greeting cards (the kind that make fun of people for getting old, or that caricature "nerds," old people, "hicks," bosses, etc.). Ask: **How do these cards put people down? Which ones do you think are funny?** After listening to responses, ask: **If put-downs were suddenly banned at your school, how would it affect conversations? What kinds of people are the most likely targets of put-downs in your school?** Read Matthew 5:21, 22. Ask: **What's the big deal about saying *raca*, which may mean "empty head," to someone? What does this passage tell you about how *not* to deal with conflicts over style?** Read Isaiah 5:21. Ask: **If a put-down is clever, does that make it OK? Explain.** Read Proverbs 22:10. Ask: **Why do people mock those who are different from themselves? What's the result?** Read James 3:9, 10. Ask: **What does this passage say about those who put others down?**

Step 5

Why not avoid everyone you don't like? Challenge complacent kids with the following activity. Have them "taste test" baby food that's spread on crackers, rating it from 1 to 5—with 5 being "delicious." Ask: **When you were little, what did you do when offered food you didn't like, or that was new to you?** (Refused to eat it; yelled; spit it out.) **How did you finally learn to eat some of those things?** (Tried and liked them; parents bribed me; tastes changed; etc.) Note that rejecting people because they're unfamiliar or "icky" is an immature response. Learning to appreciate other "flavors" of people is part of growing up spiritually as well as emotionally.

Step 3

Replace the Acts 15 study with a more easily applied passage that needs less explanation. Read the parable of the Good Samaritan (Luke 10:25-37). Then have teams act it out, updating it by making the victim someone with a style not popular in your group (a "redneck," a heavy metal fan, a computer "geek," someone who only wants to sing old hymns, etc.) and the three passersby representatives of more popular styles (rock fans, jocks, college-bound students, etc.). Ask: **Have you ever helped or been helped by someone whose style, economic level, or race differed from yours? What happened? When it comes to style, how do we try to narrow the definition of who our neighbors are? What might be the costs of reaching out to someone who has a different style? What might be the rewards?**

Step 4

Kids may wonder whether the Matthew 7 passage means they shouldn't say anything negative about anyone's immoral behavior, strange teachings, etc. Point out that if that were the case, Jesus wouldn't have warned people in the same chapter to evaluate whether prophets are false or not (vss. 15, 16). Christians are to learn to tell the difference between right and wrong behavior and true and false teachings (I Corinthians 5:9-11; I Thessalonians 5:21, 22)—in order to avoid falling into traps ourselves, and to restore believers who are stuck in sin. We are *not* to spend time on others' faults at the expense of correcting our own (Romans 2:1-4).

Step 1

Try worshiping in a style that your group isn't used to. If you usually sing choruses, sing only old hymns (or vice versa). If you generally sing with accompaniment, sing a cappella (or vice versa). If you usually stand, sit (or vice versa). Add or subtract hand clapping or hand raising if possible. If you never take an offering, take one. Then discuss how it felt. What styles of worship do your kids like? How do they feel about Christians who worship differently? Explain that you'll be discussing how to handle differences in style.

Step 5

Have kids pair up. Each partner should find out one thing that he or she doesn't know how to do that the other partner knows how to do (pass a football, speak Spanish, do a bird call, change a spark plug, etc.). Each partner will teach the other how to do that thing (or at least explain how). Then partners will explain to each other why they like to do these things, and make an effort to understand each other's interests.

Step 3
Read Acts 10:34 and talk about how Peter's support of the Gentiles included his realization that God does not have favorites. Read Galatians 3:28, 29. Say: **Since it is human nature to enjoy being with those who think and act the same way we do, how can we keep from having "favorites" among the people we know? As we follow God's example not to have favorites, does this mean we are not to have special friends? Why or why not?** Talk about some specific ways to avoid having favorites and to show God's love to every style of people.

Step 4
As you distribute "You Make the Call" (Repro Resource 9), have group members form four teams. Assign each team one of the situations on the sheet. Change the names in situation 1 to Myrna and Cheryl and in situation 4 to Katie. Then have each team read its Bible passage and plan how to act out its situation for the entire group. Each team should prepare and present two different endings. One ending should be an inappropriate, un-Christlike response to the situation. The second ending should be based on the team's research of Scripture.

Step 4
The answer to Situation 4 may seem gutless to many guys. After all, do you have to let people who can't play be on your team? How can you win that way? Note that in some cases Jesus preferred certain people over others. For example, He called only twelve to be His disciples. But His mission was more crucial than that of a church softball team. In the case of the team, the question may be: Which is more important for a church team, winning or being an example of how Christians should get along? People may disagree over the answer to that question. But putting God's kingdom first (Matthew 6:33) should help us decide when it's more important to reach a goal even if feelings are hurt, and when it's more important to maintain unity even if another goal isn't reached.

Step 5
Guys may appreciate a less "touchy-feely" application. Bring several kinds of magazines, mainly those that most guys won't like (*Family Circle, Woman's Day, Highlights for Children, Parents, Modern Maturity, Working Mother, The Writer, TeenBeat, Smithsonian, Today's Christian Woman,* etc.). Give each person a magazine he wouldn't normally read. Say: **Look through your magazine for a couple of minutes. Try to identify with someone who does like that magazine. What might his or her worries be? What might be really important to him or her? Try to find at least one thing of value in your magazine and tell the rest of us what it is.** Use this as an example of how we can—and should—try to understand and get along with those whose styles differ from our own.

Step 1
Have a sing-along led by two guitarists, each leading half the group. Try singing two different songs at the same time. Then sing the same song, but using different styles (one country, one calypso, etc.). Next, sing as a round a song that wasn't designed to be sung as a round (such as "We Are the World" or "The Ants Go Marching One by One." Finally, race each other to see which side can get through a song first. Use the disharmony as an example of what can happen when people with different styles work together—without *really* working together.

Step 5
Have an Alka-Seltzer race. Have group members form teams. Give each team a glass of water and an Alka-Seltzer tablet. At your signal, each team will plop its tablet into the water and "cheer it on" in the hope that it will be the first to dissolve completely. Give a prize to the team whose tablet dissolves first. Then explain that sometimes we need to let our styles "dissolve" into someone else's for a while in order to accomplish something important. Look at I Corinthians 9:19-23, in which Paul explains how he "became like" various kinds of non-Christians in order to win them to Christ. He didn't imitate sin, but got rid of every possible style barrier. Discuss how, in order to do that, we'd have to believe that introducing people to Jesus is more important than being comfortable all the time.

MEDIA

SHORT MEETING TIME

URBAN

Step 2

TV and movies are filled with characters whose styles clash and who are thrown together for purposes of humor or dramatic conflict. Rent one of the following movies on video. Preview and show an appropriate scene in which two of the main characters' styles clash.
• *Medicine Man* (Sean Connery vs. Lorraine Bracco)
• *Dragnet* (Dan Aykroyd vs. Tom Hanks)
• *Rain Man* (Tom Cruise vs. Dustin Hoffman)
• *Honey, I Shrunk the Kids* (Rick Moranis vs. Matt Frewer)
• *Lethal Weapon* (Mel Gibson vs. Danny Glover)
• *Indiana Jones and the Temple of Doom* (Harrison Ford vs. Kate Capshaw)
Then ask: **How would you describe each character's style? Was the conflict meant to be serious or funny? Which of the characters would you find it harder to get along with? Why?**

Step 3

Before the Bible study, play a song that reflects the world's desire for people to get along. If you can't find current examples, here are some older ones you might use: "All You Need Is Love" (The Beatles), "Everything Is Beautiful" (Ray Stevens), "Ebony and Ivory" (Paul McCartney and Michael Jackson), "Blowin' in the Wind" (Peter, Paul, and Mary). Then ask: **Did this song "ring true" for you? Why or why not? Did it offer any real advice on how people with differences can get along? If so, what was it?**

Step 1

Try an opener combining Steps 1 and 2. Before the session, rent any appropriate movie on video. Write the following on slips of paper and hand the slips to selected kids as they enter: (1) "During the movie, laugh loudly and obnoxiously at all the wrong times." (2) "During the movie, keep telling the person next to you how you've seen the movie before and what happens at the end." (3) "During the movie, keep asking the person next to you what's going on." (4) "During the movie, hold a conversation with someone a couple of rows away from you." (5) "During the movie, throw paper wads at someone in front of you." Show about two minutes of the movie while your helpers play their roles. See how others react. Then ask: **Were you ever annoyed by anybody at a movie or concert? What did you do? What did you want to do?** Ask volunteers to finish this sentence: **I just can't stand people who . . .** Pick up the basic session's Step 2 with **If it were left up to most of us . . .**

Step 3

Instead of Acts 15, study Acts 10:21-28, 34-36. Ask: **How did Cornelius treat Peter, and vice versa? What had God shown Peter about calling people impure or unclean? About favoritism? What kinds of students and teachers in your school are seen as having something "wrong" with them? What unwritten "laws" might you break by associating with them? How do conflicts over style stand in the way of spreading the Good News about Jesus at your school?** In Step 4, use just Situations 1 and 3 from the Repro Resource. Have both teams read both Bible passages. Team 1 should apply them only to Situation 1, and Team 2 should apply them only to Situation 3.

Step 2

As group members arrive, greet them wearing a bizarre array of stripes and plaids that obviously clash. Act as if this is what you actually chose to wear. Try to get the meeting started. By this time, some group members will probably be laughing or cracking jokes about your clothes. Ask those who are causing the commotion what the problem is. When they mention your clothes, tell them you put on your outfit because you liked it and didn't know it was not stylish. Ask them to point out what's wrong with your outfit so that you won't make a similar mistake again. Then explain that the session will address what happens when styles collide.

Step 3

Emphasize to your group members that disagreement is not a sin as long as it is handled correctly. Point out that truth must be sought in any disagreement. Explain that there are three ways to disagree and still search for truth:
1. Determine that the disagreement is actually agreement worded in two different ways.
2. Discuss the disagreement until it becomes an agreement.
3. Nonviolently agree to disagree.
Pair off group members and give the members of each pair a controversial topic which they must discuss maturely, using one of the disagreement resolution models.

Step 3

The church conflicts in Acts 15 may confuse and sidetrack younger kids. Use a more straightforward study. Read Galatians 3:26-28. Ask: **Does Paul mean that differences like male and female no longer exist? Explain.** (No, he means that they aren't as important as what we have in common if we're Christians—belonging to Christ.) **Based on the differences kids have today, what are some "clashing" styles you could plug into verse 28?** (Shy people and extroverts, jocks and brains, class clowns and super-serious kids, etc.) **How could this passage apply to our group?** Read Luke 9:49-56. Ask: **What do cliques usually do to someone who's "not one of us" (vs. 49)? What do you think the disciples wanted to do to the man? What did Jesus' answer mean? What did the disciples want to do to the Samaritans? What was Jesus' response? How do you usually react to people who are different from you? How would you explain that reaction to Jesus?**

Step 4

The Repro Resource situations may be slanted more toward high school than junior high. Here are two junior high situations you might use. (1) Jaleel is being driven crazy by Nick, a fellow youth group member who has a loud voice and a "donkey" laugh and who's always making "stupid" comments. It's not a big group, so Jaleel can't avoid Nick unless one of them stops going to church. What should Jaleel do? (2) Marita's in eighth grade; Elena's in sixth. They're sisters, and they have to share a room at home. Unfortunately, their styles are totally different. Marita wants to paint the walls tan, get an aquarium, and put up posters of rock groups. Elena wants the room pink, with lots of stuffed animals on the beds and nature photos on the walls. What should they do?

Step 1

If your kids would find the shoe-tying activity "beneath" them, try another option. Have pairs come up with 30-second skits—new versions of *The Odd Couple*—in which two famous characters with clashing attitudes try to share an apartment. Examples of partners group members might use include Amy Grant and Sinead O'Connor, Marky Mark and Mister Rogers, Michael Jackson and Mike Tyson, Homer Simpson and James Bond, Cher and Brooke Shields, Oscar the Grouch and Mickey Mouse. Then ask: **What personal style—messy, perfectionist, sweet, sour, etc.—would be hardest for you to live with? Why?**

Step 5

Here's a more "stretching" application. Read Romans 12:15-18. Ask: **What should be our response to those who are a lot more "up" or "down" than we are? To those who are looked down on because they're "out of it"? To those whose styles irritate or even hurt us?** Have kids write down the initials of a person they know in each of these categories: **(1) someone who is too upbeat or jokey for you, or too serious and "down"; (2) someone whose position is "lower" than yours—in age, ability, grades, income, dress, etc.; (3) someone who seems to irritate you deliberately.** Ask: **What can you do this week to live at peace with these people?**

Custom Curriculum Critique

Please take a moment to fill out this evaluation form, rip it out, fold it, tape it, and send it back to us. This will help us continue to customize products for you. Thanks!

1. Overall, please give this *Custom Curriculum* course (*You've Got Style!*) a grade in terms of how well it worked for you. (A=excellent; B=above average; C=average; D=below average; F=failure) Circle one.

$$A \quad B \quad C \quad D \quad F$$

2. Now assign a grade to each part of this curriculum that you used.

a. Upfront article	A	B	C	D	F	Didn't use
b. Publicity/Clip art	A	B	C	D	F	Didn't use
c. Repro Resource Sheets	A	B	C	D	F	Didn't use
d. Session 1	A	B	C	D	F	Didn't use
e. Session 2	A	B	C	D	F	Didn't use
f. Session 3	A	B	C	D	F	Didn't use
g. Session 4	A	B	C	D	F	Didn't use
h. Session 5	A	B	C	D	F	Didn't use

3. How helpful were the options?
   - ❑ Very helpful
   - ❑ Somewhat helpful
   - ❑ Not too helpful
   - ❑ Not at all helpful

4. Rate the amount of options:
   - ❑ Too many
   - ❑ About the right amount
   - ❑ Too few

5. Tell us how often you used each type of option (4=Always; 3=Sometimes; 2=Seldom; 1=Never)

	4	3	2	1
Extra Action	❑	❑	❑	❑
Combined Jr. High/High School	❑	❑	❑	❑
Urban	❑	❑	❑	❑
Small Group	❑	❑	❑	❑
Large Group	❑	❑	❑	❑
Extra Fun	❑	❑	❑	❑
Heard It All Before	❑	❑	❑	❑
Little Bible Background	❑	❑	❑	❑
Short Meeting Time	❑	❑	❑	❑
Fellowship and Worship	❑	❑	❑	❑
Mostly Guys	❑	❑	❑	❑
Mostly Girls	❑	❑	❑	❑
Media	❑	❑	❑	❑
Extra Challenge (High School only)	❑	❑	❑	❑
Sixth Grade (Jr. High only)	❑	❑	❑	❑

6. What did you like best about this course?

7. What suggestions do you have for improving *Custom Curriculum*?

8. Other topics you'd like to see covered in this series:

9. Are you?
   ❑ Full time paid youthworker
   ❑ Part time paid youthworker
   ❑ Volunteer youthworker

10. When did you use *Custom Curriculum*?
    ❑ Sunday School   ❑ Small Group
    ❑ Youth Group   ❑ Retreat
    ❑ Other _____

11. What grades did you use it with? _____

12. How many kids used the curriculum in an average week? _____

13. What's the approximate attendance of your entire Sunday school program (Nursery through Adult)? _____

14. If you would like information on other *Custom Curriculum* courses, or other youth products from David C. Cook, please fill out the following:

Name: _____
Church Name: _____
Address: _____
_____
Phone: (____) _____

Thank you!